The Navy SEAL Ultimate Home Defense Playbook

Proven Military Tactics to
Secure Your Family and Fortify Your Home

Real-World Strategies from a Retired SEAL to Prepare for Any Crisis

Written by Jake T. Donovan

© Copyright 2025 by Jake T. Donovan - All rights reserved.

All rights reserved. No part of this book may be reproduced, distributed, or transmitted in any form or by any means, including photocopying, recording, or other electronic or mechanical methods, without prior written permission from the author. Reviewers may quote brief passages for the purpose of reviews.

While every effort has been made to verify the information provided in this publication, neither the author nor the publisher assumes responsibility for any errors, omissions, or contrary interpretations of the subject matter contained herein.

The views expressed in this publication are solely those of the author and should not be considered as professional advice or instruction. The reader is solely responsible for their actions and interpretations of the material within this book.

Compliance with all applicable laws and regulations, including but not limited to international, federal, state, and local laws governing business practices, advertising, and professional licensing, is the sole responsibility of the reader.

Neither the author nor the publisher assumes any liability or responsibility for any errors or potential consequences resulting from the use of this material. Any perceived slight of any individual, organization, or entity is unintentional.

Table Of Contents

Introduction: Your Home as Your Fortress 12
What This Book Offers 12
Why Preparation Matters 13
How to use this book 13

Chapter 1: Think Like a Navy SEAL 14
Understanding Situational Awareness 14
The OODA Loop: A Navy SEAL's Decision-Making Tool 15
Adapting to the Unexpected 15
Exercises to Build Your SEAL Mindset 15
Expanding Your Awareness: Beyond the Basics 16
Enhancing Decision-Making Under Stress 16
Turning Preparation Into Confidence 17

Chapter 2: Preparation Is the Best Defense 18
Why You Need a Plan 18
The Psychology of Planning 18
Building Confidence Through Redundancy 19
Involving Your Family 19
Step 1: Assess Your Risks 19
Step 2: Define Your Objectives 20
Step 3: Create Your Defense Plan 21
Step 4: Test and Refine Your Plan 21
Advanced Planning Tips 22
Real-Life Example: The Value of Practice 22

Chapter 3: Conducting a Security Audit 23
Finding the Weak Spots 23
Understanding the Threat Landscape 23
Finding the Weak Spots in Everyday Activities 23
Step 1: Start at the Perimeter 24
Step 2: Entry Point Inspection 24
Step 3: Interior Security 25
Step 4: Simulate and Test Your Defenses 26
Real-Life SEAL Insight: Layered Defense Saves Lives .. 26
Taking Your Security Further 26

Chapter 4: Layers of Defense 28
Building a Multi-Layered Defense System 28

- Why Layers Matter: The Defense-in-Depth Principle ... 28
- The Role of Deterrence ... 28
- Layered Defense Beyond the Physical ... 29
- The Importance of Redundancy ... 29
- Thinking Like an Intruder ... 30
  - Layer 1: Perimeter Defense ... 30
  - Layer 2: Entry Point Reinforcement ... 31
  - Layer 3: Interior Defense ... 31
  - Layer 4: Psychological Deterrence ... 32

Chapter 5: Defensive Tools and Gear ... 33

- Tools That Make the Difference ... 33
- Beyond the Basics: The Philosophy of Gear Selection ... 33
- Integrating Tools with Your Environment ... 33
- Psychological Power of Visible Tools ... 34
- The Role of Training in Effective Tool Use ... 34
- Budgeting for Your Defense System ... 35
- Integrating Smart Technology ... 35
  - Category 1: Non-Lethal Defensive Tools ... 36
  - Category 2: Tactical Tools for Home Defense ... 36
  - Category 3: Defensive Infrastructure ... 36
- Training and Maintenance ... 37
- Real-Life SEAL Insight: Gear Is Secondary to Skill ... 37
- Equipping Your Fortress ... 37
  - Step 1: Choosing the Right Surveillance Systems ... 37
  - Step 2: Enhancing Entry Point Security ... 38
  - Step 3: Leveraging Technology for Alerts and Automation ... 38
  - Step 4: Non-Lethal Defensive Tools ... 39
  - Step 5: Emergency Supplies for Crises ... 39
  - Step 6: Regular Maintenance and Training ... 40
- Real-Life SEAL Insight ... 40

Chapter 6: Stockpiling Essentials Navy SEAL Style ... 41

- Be Ready for Anything ... 41
- Why Stockpiling Matters ... 41
- Stockpiling vs. Hoarding: The Key Differences ... 41
- Psychological Benefits of Being Prepared ... 42
- Tailoring Your Stockpile to Your Family's Needs ... 42
- Planning for Long-Term Emergencies ... 42
- Integrating Stockpiling Into Daily Life ... 43
- Stockpiling as a Community Effort ... 43
- How to stockpile correctly ... 43
  - Step 1: Identify Your Needs ... 43

- Step 2: Efficient Storage Solutions 44
- Step 3: Tactical Tips for Stockpiling Food and Water 44
- Step 4: Organize Your Stockpile 45
- Step 5: Protect Your Supplies 45
- Step 6: Stockpile Maintenance 46

Real-Life SEAL Insight: Efficient Packing Saves Lives 46

Chapter 7: Energy Independence 47

Staying Powered When the Grid Fails 47

Why Energy Independence Is Essential 47

Understanding the Scope of Energy Needs 47

The Psychological Comfort of Energy Security 48

Balancing Renewable and Non-Renewable Options 48

Planning for Long-Term Outages 48

Incorporating Energy Independence into Daily Life 49

The SEAL Mindset: Adapting and Overcoming 49

How to secure electricity 49
- Step 1: Understand Your Energy Needs 49
- Step 2: Choose Your Power Sources 50
- Step 3: Store Energy Effectively 51
- Step 4: Optimize Energy Usage 51
- Step 5: Water and Waste Systems 52
- Step 6: Maintain Your Systems 52

Real-Life SEAL Insight: Redundancy Equals Resilience 52

Chapter 8: Medical Preparedness 53

When Every Second Counts 53

Why Medical Preparedness Is Critical 53

The Psychological Impact of Being Prepared 53

Tailoring Preparedness to Your Family's Needs 53

Integrating Medical Preparedness Into Daily Life 54

The Role of Community in Medical Preparedness 54

Adapting to Long-Term Medical Challenges 55

How to make sure you can cope with medical emergencies 55
- Step 1: Build a Professional-Grade First Aid Kit 55
- Step 2: Address Common Medical Emergencies 56
- Step 3: Store and Protect Medical Supplies 56
- Step 4: Acquire Essential Medical Skills 57
- Step 5: Plan for Long-Term Medical Needs 57
- Step 6: Teach and Involve Your Family 57

Real-Life SEAL Insight: Training Saves Lives 58

Chapter 9: Actionable Defense Tactics 59

Staying Ready in High-Stakes Moments 59

The Importance of Situational Readiness 59
Building Confidence Through Preparation 59
Leveraging Your Environment 60
Psychological Deterrence 60
Understanding the Psychology of Intruders 60
Key Principles to Remember 61
How to make sure you are prepared for danger 61
    Step 1: Recognize the Signs of Trouble 61
    Step 2: Defensive Positioning in Your Home 61
    Step 3: De-escalation Strategies 62
    Step 4: Defensive Tools and Their Use 62
    Step 5: Family Coordination and Roles 62
    Step 6: When Confrontation Is Unavoidable 63
Real-Life SEAL Insight: Clarity Under Pressure 63

Chapter 10: Resilience and Recovery 64

Bouncing Back After a Crisis 64
The Multifaceted Nature of Recovery 64
The Psychological Aftermath of Emergencies 64
Turning Lessons Into Strength 65
Strengthening Bonds Through Recovery 65
Engaging Your Community in Recovery 65
How to Rebuild Resilience After a Crisis 66
    Step 1: Assess the Damage 66
    Step 2: Strengthen Your Home's Defenses 66
    Step 3: Rebuild Trust and Routine 67
    Step 4: Manage Financial and Logistical Recovery 67
    Step 5: Foster Psychological Resilience 67
    Step 6: Stay Prepared for the Future 68

Chapter 11: Advanced SEAL Tactics for Home Defense 69

Taking Home Defense to the Next Level 69
The SEAL Approach to Mastery 69
Transforming Your Home into a Tactical Asset 69
Mental Toughness: The Ultimate Defense 70
How to Implement Advanced SEAL Tactics for Home Defense 70
    Step 1: Develop Situational Awareness on a New Level 70
    Step 2: Secure Your Home with Redundant Layers 71
    Step 3: Master Tactical Movement in Your Home 71
    Step 4: Establish Offense as a Last Resort 71
    Step 5: Engage in Advanced Drills and Training 72
    Step 6: Consider Intelligence Gathering 72
    Real-Life SEAL Insight: Planning for the Worst-Case Scenario 72

Chapter 12: DIY Projects for Food Independence 73

Crafting a Resilient Home 73

Redefining Home Independence 73

The DIY Mindset: Turning Challenges into Opportunities 73

Empowering Your Family Through DIY Projects 74

How to Build a Resilient Home with DIY Projects 74
    Step 1: Water Independence with DIY Collection and Filtration Systems 74
    Step 2: Generate Your Own Power 75
    Step 3: Grow Your Own Food with Vertical Gardening 76
    Step 4: Build a DIY Backup Heating System 76

Projects to secure food 77
    Step 1: Build Raised Garden Beds 77
    Step 2: Start a Small-Scale Livestock Project 77
    Step 3: Preserve Your Harvest 79
    Step 4: Incorporate Aquaponics 79

Chapter 13: Energy Efficiency for Sustainable Living 81

Maximizing Efficiency for Resilient Homes 81

The Importance of Energy Efficiency in a Crisis 81

Key Benefits of an Energy-Efficient Home 81

Common Energy Wastes in Homes 82

Setting Energy Efficiency Goals 82

Breaking Down Energy Efficiency by Zones 82

Building a Holistic Approach 83

How to: Transform Your Home into an Energy-Efficient Powerhouse 83
    Step 1: Improve Home Insulation 83
    Step 2: Install Energy-Efficient Lighting 83
    Step 3: Optimize Heating and Cooling Systems 84
    Step 4: Integrate Renewable Energy Sources 84
    Step 5: Harvest Passive Energy 85
    Step 6: Reduce Phantom Energy 85

Chapter 14: Mastering Water Management for Total Independence 87

The Lifeblood of Self-Sufficiency 87

Expanding Beyond the Basics 87
    1. Understanding Water Availability 87
    2. Integrating Water Management into Everyday Life 87
    3. Anticipating Challenges 87

Innovative Water Management Concepts 88
    1. Advanced Rainwater Harvesting Techniques 88
    2. Greywater Integration into a Closed-Loop System 88
    3. Emergency Water Sources and Strategies 88

How to Master Water Management for Total Independence 88
    Step 1: Evaluate Your Water Needs 88
    Step 2: Build a Resilient Water Collection System 89
    Step 3: Purify Water for Safe Consumption 89
    Step 4: Store Water Safely 89
    Step 5: Optimize Usage During Emergencies 90

Chapter 15: Creating a Fully Self-Sufficient Home Ecosystem 91

Designing for Independence 91
Expanding Your Vision of Independence 91
   1. Holistic Resource Management 91
   2. Anticipating Environmental Challenges 91
   3. Futureproofing Through Scalable Systems 91
How to Design a Self-Sufficient Home Ecosystem 92
   Step 1: Assess Your Home's Capabilities 92
   Step 2: Build Integrated Energy Systems 92
   Step 3: Develop Sustainable Water Systems 93
   Step 4: Establish Self-Sustaining Food Production 93
   Step 5: Implement Efficient Waste Management 94
   Step 6: Integrate Smart Home Technology 95

Chapter 16: Advanced Strategies for Long-Term Resilience 96

Thriving in the Face of Uncertainty 96
Beyond Basics: The Resilience Mindset 96
How to Implement Advanced Strategies for Long-Term Resilience 97
   Step 1: Develop a Long-Term Resource Plan 97
   Step 2: Master Advanced Food Production Techniques 97
   Step 3: Strengthen Community Connections 98
   Step 4: Prepare for Worst-Case Scenarios 98
   Step 5: Regularly Test and Adapt Your Systems 99

Chapter 17: Scaling Your Self-Sufficient Lifestyle 101

Beyond Your Four Walls 101
Why Scale Your Self-Sufficient Lifestyle? 101
Key Areas for Expansion 101
   1. Food Production: From Backyard to Homestead 101
   2. Energy Systems: Scaling Sustainability 102
   3. Bartering and Local Economies 102
   4. Knowledge Sharing and Education 102
Community as a Foundation for Scaling 103
   The Power of Collective Resilience 103
   Real-Life Inspiration 103
How to Expand Your Self-Sufficient Lifestyle and Build Community Resilience 103
   Step 1: Expand Food Production Systems 103
   Step 2: Enhance Renewable Energy Systems 104
   Step 3: Establish a Bartering Economy 105
   Step 4: Teach and Inspire Others 105
   Step 5: Advocate for Community Resilience 106

Chapter 18: Integrating Modern Technology with Self-Sufficient Practices 107

Bridging the Gap Between Tradition and Innovation 107
The Advantages of Tech-Enhanced Self-Sufficiency 107
Core Principles of Tech Integration 107
   1. Efficiency Without Dependency 107
   2. Modular Design for Flexibility 108
   3. Data as a Tool for Growth 108

Technology in Practice: Key Applications 108
Energy Systems 108
Food Production 108
Water Management 108

Real-Life Examples of Tech-Enhanced Practices 109

Challenges and Solutions in Tech Integration 109
Challenge 1: Initial Costs 109
Challenge 2: Technology Overload 109
Challenge 3: Maintenance Complexity 109

Future-Proofing Your Tech Integration 109
Adopt Emerging Technologies 109
Community-Based Solutions 110
Sustainable Upgrades 110

How to Integrate Technology with Self-Sufficient Practices 110
Step 1: Leverage Smart Home Technology 110
Step 2: Utilize Advanced Renewable Energy Systems 111
Step 3: Integrate Hydroponics and Automation 111
Step 4: Explore Cutting-Edge Water Management Tools 112
Step 5: Embrace Data-Driven Decision Making 112

Chapter 19: Building a Legacy of Preparedness *114*

Introduction: Passing the Torch 114

The Importance of Legacy in Preparedness 114

Core Principles for Creating a Lasting Legacy 114
1. Lead by Example 114
2. Focus on Knowledge Transfer 114
3. Build Adaptable Systems 115

Key Areas for Legacy Building 115
1. Education Across Generations 115
2. Durable, Scalable Systems 115
3. Community Engagement 115

Real-Life Inspirations 115

How to Build a Legacy of Preparedness 116
Step 1: Educate the Next Generation 116
Step 2: Build Durable Systems 116
Step 3: Create a Preparedness Culture 117
Step 4: Pass Down Your Knowledge 117
Step 5: Inspire Future Generations 118

Chapter 20: Advanced Survival Scenarios and Strategies *120*

Thriving in the Unpredictable 120

Beyond Basic Preparedness 120
1. Expanding Your Toolkit 120
2. Strategic Mindset 120
3. Building Mental and Emotional Resilience 120

Core Advanced Strategies 121
1. Proactive Planning 121
2. Tactical Resource Management 121
3. Training for Real-World Scenarios 121

How to Navigate Advanced Survival Scenarios and Strategies 121
- Step 1: Prolonged Power Outages 121
- Step 2: Natural Disasters 122
- Step 3: Civil Unrest 122
- Step 4: Extended Isolation 123
- Step 5: Advanced Medical Preparedness 124

Chapter 21: The Economics of Self-Sufficiency *125*

Introduction: Financial Independence Through Sustainability 125

The Financial Case for Self-Sufficiency 125
- 1. Breaking Free from Rising Costs 125
- 2. Turning Savings Into Investments 125
- 3. Contributing to a Circular Economy 125

How to Master the Economics of Self-Sufficiency 126
- Step 1: Analyze Cost Savings 126
- Step 2: Generate Income From Surplus Resources 126
- Step 3: Invest in Durable Systems 127
- Step 4: Leverage Tax Incentives and Grants 128
- Step 5: Plan for Financial Resilience 128

Chapter 22: Preparing for a Sustainable Future *130*

Introduction: Shaping Tomorrow Today 130

The Path to Sustainable Resilience 130
- Why Sustainability Matters 130

How to Prepare for a Sustainable Future 130
- Step 1: Understand Future Challenges 130
- Step 2: Innovate for Sustainability 131
- Step 3: Build Collaborative Networks 131
- Step 4: Prioritize Environmental Stewardship 132
- Step 5: Plan for Future Generations 133

Rebuilding for a Resilient Future 133
- Step 1: Assess the Damage 134
- Step 2: Secure Essential Needs 134
- Step 3: Develop a Recovery Plan 135
- Step 4: Foster Emotional and Mental Recovery 135
- Step 5: Build Back Better 136

Chapter 23: Cybersecurity for Home Defense *138*

Protecting Your Digital Fortress 138

Common Cybersecurity Threats 138
- Phishing Attacks, Malware, and Ransomware 138
- Risks from Unsecured Smart Devices 138
- Data Theft and Financial Fraud 138

Building Digital Defenses 139
- Creating Strong Passwords and Using Password Managers 139
- Setting Up a VPN 139
- Installing and Updating Firewalls and Antivirus Software 139
- Securing IoT Devices 139

Recognizing and Responding to Threats 139
- How to Identify Phishing Attempts and Suspicious Activities 139
- Steps to Take During a Cybersecurity Breach 140

Resources for Monitoring and Reporting Threats 140
Pro Tip: Schedule monthly cybersecurity checkups to review settings, update devices, and ensure all systems are operating with the latest security protocols. These small, consistent actions can significantly reduce vulnerabilities and keep your digital fortress secure. 140

Chapter 24: Fitness and Training for Preparedness............................ 141

Introduction: Strength and Resilience for Survival..**141**
The Role of Fitness in Preparedness...**141**
Why Physical Fitness Matters 141
Designing a Preparedness Fitness Plan..**141**
Key Components of a Balanced Routine 141
Preparedness-Specific Workouts..**142**
Functional Training Routine 142
Real-Life Training Scenarios..**142**
Scenario 1: Bug-Out Practice 142
Scenario 2: Defensive Position Drills..142
Scenario 3: Lifting and Carrying 142
Monitoring Progress and Staying Motivated..**142**
Tracking Fitness Improvements 142
Staying Committed...143
Pro Tip: Every small improvement in fitness can significantly enhance your survival odds in a crisis. Regularly update your fitness plan to align with your evolving preparedness needs. 143
4-Week Preparedness Fitness Plan **143**
Week 1: Foundation Building 143
Week 2: Progression...144
Week 3: Tactical Training 144
Week 4: Peak Challenge 145

Chapter 25: Expanding Defense to Vehicles 146

Mobile Security as a Strategic Asset..**146**
Securing Your Vehicle **146**
Preparing Your Vehicle for Emergencies **146**
Using Vehicles as Part of Your Defense Strategy **147**
Maintenance and Long-Term Preparation..**147**
Real-Life Example **148**

Conclusion: A Legacy of Resilience and Preparedness........................ 149

Preparedness Is Empowerment **149**
Beyond the Individual: Building a Culture of Resilience **149**
A Future Ready for Anything...**149**

Unlock Exclusive Bonuses!.. 151

A Personal Note of Thanks 152

Introduction: Your Home as Your Fortress

When I was a Navy SEAL, we were taught to see the world differently. Every building was a potential stronghold or a trap. Every moment demanded vigilance. At its heart, our training wasn't about weapons or tactics—it was about mindset. That same mindset can transform your home from just a place to live into a fortress capable of withstanding crises of any kind.

The truth is, we live in uncertain times. Natural disasters, break-ins, and social unrest can strike without warning. But here's the good news: you don't have to be a Navy SEAL to protect your family. You just need the right guidance, a clear plan, and the determination to act before it's too late.

This book is about more than security cameras or locks. It's about adopting a way of thinking that combines preparation, adaptability, and confidence. Along the way, I'll share stories from my time as a SEAL, lessons learned in high-stakes environments, and practical strategies you can use to secure your home and safeguard your loved ones.

Let me give you an example. In 2003, while deployed in a hostile region, my team was tasked with securing an abandoned building and using it as a temporary base. The building was in poor shape—doors off hinges, shattered windows, and no power. But within hours, we turned that wreck into a defensible stronghold by layering our defenses, planning for contingencies, and working as a team. The principles we used then are the same ones you'll find in these pages.

What This Book Offers

This book isn't about turning you into a soldier. It's about equipping you with practical, easy-to-follow strategies to prepare for emergencies, secure your home, and maintain peace of mind. From conducting a security audit to managing energy independence, each chapter is designed to give you actionable steps without overwhelming jargon or unnecessary theory.

You'll learn how to:

- Think like a Navy SEAL, applying situational awareness and adaptability to your everyday life.
- Conduct a step-by-step audit of your home's vulnerabilities.
- Build layered defenses that deter, delay, and neutralize threats.
- Prepare for crises with stockpiles, medical kits, and energy solutions.
- Protect your family during emergencies with tactical, real-world strategies.

Why Preparation Matters

I've seen firsthand what happens when people are unprepared. In one operation, we were called in to assist after a local community was devastated by a flood. Homes were destroyed, people were stranded, and resources were scarce. Those who had prepared—even minimally—fared much better. They had food, clean water, and the means to communicate or evacuate. The unprepared? They were left vulnerable, relying on the slow arrival of outside help.

Preparation isn't about fear; it's about control. It's about ensuring that, when the unexpected happens, you're ready to act, not react.

How to use this book

Each chapter builds on the last, providing a logical progression from mindset to action. By the time you finish, you'll have a comprehensive plan tailored to your home and family's needs. Think of this book as your personal guide to building a fortress—not a castle of stone and mortar, but a safe haven created through smart planning, practical tools, and unwavering confidence.

Let's begin. Your home is your fortress, and you are its first and best line of defense.

Chapter 1: Think Like a Navy SEAL

When I first started SEAL training, I didn't know what to expect. I had the physical skills, but I quickly realized the true challenge was mental. We weren't just taught to act; we were taught to think—to analyze situations, anticipate threats, and stay calm under pressure. This mindset is the foundation of everything we did, and it's the first step in turning your home into a fortress.

The SEAL mindset isn't about fear—it's about control. It's the ability to remain level-headed in chaos, to identify opportunities in adversity, and to make decisive choices when seconds matter. Let's explore how you can adopt this approach in your everyday life and use it to secure your home.

Understanding Situational Awareness

Imagine you're sitting in your living room one evening. The lights are dim, the TV is on, and you're scrolling through your phone. Outside, a car drives past slowly. Do you notice it? Is it the first time that car has passed, or the third? This small observation could be the difference between recognizing a potential threat and missing it entirely.

Situational awareness is about noticing these details. It's the ability to scan your surroundings, identify anything out of the ordinary, and assess its potential as a threat. It's not about paranoia—it's about being present and observant.

Here's how you can practice it:

- **Start Small:** When you walk into a room, take a few seconds to notice the exits, the people, and any potential hazards. Ask yourself questions like, "Where are the windows?" or "What's within reach that could be used to defend myself?"
- **Observe Patterns:** In your neighborhood, pay attention to the usual rhythm—when people come and go, which cars belong, and which don't. Over time, you'll start to notice when something feels out of place.
- **Teach Your Family:** Make situational awareness a shared habit. Turn it into a game for kids—ask them to spot five things that have changed in a room, or to identify escape routes in public spaces like restaurants or malls.

Real-Life Example: During a mission overseas, my team always conducted reconnaissance before entering a building. We observed from a distance, noting every window, door, and unusual detail. This allowed us to anticipate risks and plan accordingly. At home, this same approach can help you spot vulnerabilities before they become problems, such as a broken lock or a poorly lit entryway.

The OODA Loop: A Navy SEAL's Decision-Making Tool

SEALs rely on a simple but powerful process called the OODA Loop—Observe, Orient, Decide, Act. This cycle helps us process information quickly and respond effectively in any situation. Here's how it works:

1. **Observe:** Take in the situation. For home defense, this might mean noticing an unfamiliar car parked near your house or a stranger lingering near your property.
2. **Orient:** Analyze what you've observed. Is the car just a neighbor's guest, or is it out of place? Is the stranger lost, or are they behaving suspiciously?
3. **Decide:** Choose your action. Maybe you jot down the license plate, notify your family, or keep an eye on the situation.
4. **Act:** Follow through. If the situation escalates, you might call law enforcement or move your family to a safe room.

Real-Life Example: During a training exercise, I once hesitated between two decisions—approach a building or wait for backup. That hesitation cost us valuable time and nearly compromised the mission. The OODA Loop teaches you to process quickly and act decisively, a skill you can apply to defending your home.

Adapting to the Unexpected

The hallmark of a SEAL is adaptability. Plans change, conditions shift, and the ability to think on your feet is what keeps you alive. The same is true for home defense.

Let's say your neighborhood experiences a power outage during a storm. Suddenly, your alarm system is offline, and your home feels exposed. What's your plan?

- **Backup Systems:** Have battery-powered or solar chargers for critical devices.
- **Low-Tech Solutions:** Keep flashlights, candles, and manual locks ready.
- **Stay Calm:** Panicking only makes the situation worse. Take a moment to assess your options before acting.

I've been in situations where our primary plan fell apart—like when a helicopter extraction was delayed, forcing us to improvise an escape. Those experiences taught me that preparation is only part of the equation; adaptability is just as important.

Real-Life Example: On a deployment, a helicopter extraction was delayed, forcing us to improvise an escape. Our ability to adapt—finding alternative routes and working together—was what kept us safe. At home, adaptability could mean anything from changing escape plans during a fire to handling a prolonged power outage.

Exercises to Build Your SEAL Mindset

To develop a SEAL-like mindset, you need to practice daily. Here are a few exercises:

- **Daily Awareness Practice:** Spend 5 minutes a day observing your environment. Note anything unusual—like an open gate, unfamiliar footsteps, or a burnt-out streetlight near your property.
- **Scenario Rehearsals:** Imagine different crises, such as a break-in, fire, or severe weather. Walk through your response step by step, and involve your family in these rehearsals.
- **Stress Training:** Put yourself in controlled, high-pressure situations to improve your ability to think clearly under stress. For example, try solving puzzles or completing tasks with a timer to simulate the urgency of real-life crises.

Real-Life Example: A homeowner I worked with practiced regular drills for fire and break-in scenarios with their family. When a minor kitchen fire broke out one evening, their kids knew exactly what to do—grab the fire extinguisher, call 911, and evacuate calmly. Their preparation turned a potentially dangerous situation into a controlled one.

Expanding Your Awareness: Beyond the Basics

Situational awareness doesn't end with your immediate environment; it's a skill that extends to your broader community. For instance, learn the patterns of activity in your neighborhood. Is there an area where loitering often occurs? Are there frequent break-ins reported near certain intersections? By understanding these external factors, you'll be better prepared to anticipate potential risks and act accordingly.

- **Engage with Local Networks:** Join neighborhood watch programs or social media groups where residents share updates about suspicious activities.
- **Stay Informed:** Regularly check local news and crime reports to understand emerging trends.
- **Conduct Walkabouts:** Periodically walk around your property and nearby areas to identify new vulnerabilities or changes in the environment.

Real-Life Example: A homeowner noticed an abandoned vehicle near their property for several days. By contacting local authorities and coordinating with neighbors, they discovered it was linked to a series of thefts, helping prevent future incidents.

Enhancing Decision-Making Under Stress

Stress can cloud judgment, especially in high-stakes situations. Training your mind to process information clearly, even under pressure, is vital for effective decision-making.

- **Simulate Scenarios:** Practice responding to different crises, like a break-in or fire, by running timed drills. Include obstacles to replicate real-world challenges.
- **Use Controlled Breathing Techniques:** Slow, deep breaths help lower your heart rate and improve focus. Practice this during daily tasks to make it a habit.
- **Focus on Micro-Decisions:** Break larger problems into smaller, actionable steps. For example, during a fire, your immediate steps might be to alert family members, grab an extinguisher, and head to your designated safe zone.

Real-Life Example: A friend experienced a sudden house fire caused by faulty wiring. Their ability to stay calm, evacuate their family, and call emergency services stemmed directly from practicing drills and focusing on one task at a time.

Turning Preparation Into Confidence

As you develop these skills, you'll notice a shift in how you approach daily life. Instead of feeling overwhelmed by potential threats, you'll gain a sense of control and confidence. This transformation is the essence of the SEAL mindset: preparation not for fear, but for empowerment. It's about knowing that no matter what comes your way, you'll have the tools and mental clarity to face it head-on.

Real-Life Example: A homeowner who adopted SEAL-inspired practices reported feeling a greater sense of security, not just at home but also in public spaces. By combining situational awareness with rehearsed responses, they felt equipped to handle challenges ranging from minor disturbances to significant emergencies.

Adopting the SEAL mindset isn't about turning your home into a war zone. It's about creating a calm, confident approach to life that prepares you for the unexpected. By practicing situational awareness, mastering the OODA Loop, and developing adaptability, you're laying the foundation for a secure and resilient home. The next chapter will build on this foundation, guiding you through the steps of creating a personalized home defense plan.

Chapter 2: Preparation Is the Best Defense

In the Navy SEALs, we had a saying: "Failing to plan is planning to fail." No matter how skilled or strong you are, without a plan, you're vulnerable. This chapter is about building a customized home defense plan that addresses your unique needs and sets you up for success in any crisis. Whether it's a natural disaster, a break-in, or a prolonged power outage, preparation can mean the difference between chaos and control.

Why You Need a Plan

Imagine this: It's 2 a.m., and you hear glass shattering downstairs. Adrenaline kicks in, and your mind races. What do you do? Do you grab your phone? Lock your bedroom door? Confront the intruder? Without a plan, you're relying on instinct and luck—and those are unreliable in high-stress situations.

A well-thought-out defense plan gives you clear actions to follow, reducing panic and increasing your chances of protecting your family. But a plan is more than just knowing what to do; it's about aligning your actions with your environment, your risks, and your family's specific needs. Let's break this down step by step.

The Psychology of Planning

When we plan for potential threats, we're not just preparing physically—we're conditioning our minds. In high-stress situations, your brain naturally defaults to its most rehearsed responses. If you've never practiced what to do in an emergency, you're likely to freeze or make hasty, irrational decisions. A solid plan combats this by providing clarity and structure.

Consider this: when your family rehearses fire drills, they're not just learning where to go—they're learning how to override panic with purposeful action. This psychological advantage can mean the difference between a calm evacuation and chaos.

Real-Life Example: During a neighborhood blackout, one family I worked with executed their power outage plan seamlessly. They immediately switched to battery-powered lighting, set up their backup generator, and ensured all family members knew which devices to prioritize. Their planning eliminated panic and allowed them to focus on staying safe.

Building Confidence Through Redundancy

One of the key principles we learned in SEAL training was redundancy: always have a backup plan for your backup plan. This principle is equally vital in home defense. For instance:

- If your primary escape route is blocked, do you have a secondary and tertiary route?
- If your main safe room becomes inaccessible, is there an alternative location where your family can gather?
- If your phone battery dies, do you have a pre-arranged way to contact emergency services?

Redundancy ensures that even if one system fails, your overall plan remains intact. It's better to have multiple layers of security and never need them than to find yourself exposed when a single point of failure collapses.

Pro Tip: Walk through your home and identify all possible escape routes and safe zones. Don't just focus on obvious options—think creatively about windows, secondary doors, or even climbing over a fence to a neighbor's yard if necessary.

Involving Your Family

Preparation is a team effort. Every member of your household, from children to elderly relatives, should have a role in your defense plan. Here's how to involve them:

1. **Age-Appropriate Training:**
   - Young children can learn simple actions like crawling low to avoid smoke or recognizing safe adults to approach in a crisis.
   - Teenagers can take on more complex responsibilities, such as managing emergency communication tools or assisting with younger siblings.
2. **Family Meetings:**
   - Regularly discuss potential scenarios and ensure everyone understands their role. Use clear, simple language to avoid confusion.
   - Create a checklist for each person, such as "grab the go-bag" or "ensure the doors are locked."
3. **Rehearsal Drills:**
   - Schedule monthly practice sessions for different emergencies. For instance, simulate a break-in one month and an earthquake the next.
   - Include contingencies, like what to do if one family member is away or unable to follow the plan.

Real-Life Example: A family I trained created a "buddy system" where each child was paired with an adult during emergencies. This ensured no one was left behind, and younger kids felt reassured knowing they had a specific person to rely on.

Step 1: Assess Your Risks

Not all threats are created equal. Your plan should be tailored to the specific risks you face. Consider the following:

- **Geographic Risks:**
    - If you live in a hurricane-prone area, focus on securing windows, waterproofing critical areas, and having an evacuation plan.
    - In wildfire zones, prioritize defensible space around your home by clearing vegetation, and have fire-resistant materials on hand.
    - Earthquake-prone regions require bolting furniture to walls, securing gas lines, and preparing for extended disruptions.
- **Lifestyle Factors:**
    - Do you leave the house empty during work hours? Set timers for lights and consider installing remote monitoring systems.
    - Do you have young children? Ensure safety measures like locking cabinets and securing sharp objects are in place.
    - Are there elderly or disabled family members? Create mobility-friendly escape routes and stock extra medical supplies.
- **Neighborhood Insights:**
    - Talk to your neighbors and neighborhood watch groups to understand local crime patterns.
    - Use crime mapping tools online to identify recent trends in your area, such as car theft or vandalism.

Real-Life Example: I once worked with a family in a suburban area who thought their biggest risk was burglary. After reviewing their setup, we realized their poorly maintained landscaping was a fire hazard during dry seasons—something they hadn't considered. Addressing both risks improved their overall preparedness.

Checklist: Risk Assessment Factors

1. Identify natural disaster risks (floods, fires, earthquakes).
2. Evaluate local crime trends (break-ins, vandalism, car theft).
3. Consider family-specific needs (children, pets, medical conditions).
4. Review potential utility failures (water, gas, electricity).

Step 2: Define Your Objectives

Once you understand your risks, you can define clear goals for your plan. Ask yourself:

- **What are you protecting?** Your family, valuables, or property?
- **Against what threats?** Intruders, natural disasters, or power outages?
- **What are your priorities?** Is your focus on evacuation, deterrence, or confrontation?

Example Scenarios:

- A single mother with two children might prioritize creating a safe room, ensuring it's stocked with communication tools, water, and first aid supplies, and practicing evacuation routes.

- A retired couple in a rural area might focus on securing entry points, installing motion-activated lights, and stockpiling food and water for extended isolation during emergencies.

Pro Tip: Write down your objectives and revisit them periodically to ensure they align with changing circumstances.

Step 3: Create Your Defense Plan

Your plan should address multiple scenarios and be easy to follow for every family member. Here are the key elements:

- **Evacuation Routes:** Identify the fastest and safest ways out of your home. Mark these routes on a floor plan and practice using them during drills. For multi-story homes, consider escape ladders for upper floors.
- **Safe Zones:** Designate areas in your home where your family can gather during emergencies. A reinforced safe room with a solid-core door, communication devices, and essential supplies is ideal.
- **Communication:** Establish a family contact plan. Include primary and backup methods, such as texting, phone calls, or walkie-talkies. Designate a meeting point outside the home in case of evacuation.
- **Defense Measures:** Detail how you'll respond to specific threats:
  - **Break-In:** Lock doors, gather in the safe room, and alert authorities.
  - **Fire:** Follow evacuation routes, turn off gas if safe to do so, and call 911.
  - **Power Outage:** Use backup power systems to maintain critical functions and stay updated via battery-powered radios.

Real-Life Example: When my team was deployed to secure a high-risk compound, our plan included multiple entry and exit routes, fallback positions, and protocols for every conceivable scenario. At home, the same principles apply: redundancy and clarity.

Step 4: Test and Refine Your Plan

A plan is only as good as its execution. Regular testing ensures everyone knows their role and identifies weak points.

- **Family Drills:** Practice responses to common threats, like evacuating during a fire or locking down during a break-in.
- **Review and Adjust:** Life changes—new neighbors, renovations, or evolving risks mean your plan needs to evolve too.
- **Document Your Plan:** Write it down and share it with every family member. Keep a copy in your safe room and another in a secure digital location.

Advanced Planning Tips

- **Redundancy:** Have backup options for everything. If your primary escape route is blocked, know your secondary and tertiary options. If your main safe room is compromised, identify another fallback location.
- **Community Integration:** Coordinate with trusted neighbors to share resources and support during emergencies. For example, one family might have medical supplies while another has a generator.
- **Tech Integration:** Use smart home devices like doorbell cameras, motion sensors, and remote locks to enhance your defense plan. Set alerts on your phone to notify you of unusual activity when you're away.

Real-Life Example: The Value of Practice

I once worked with a homeowner who wanted to improve his family's preparedness for break-ins. We ran a mock drill, simulating a nighttime intrusion. During the drill, they realized their safe room was poorly stocked and their children didn't know how to lock the door. These issues were easily fixed, but only because they tested their plan.

Preparation isn't a one-time effort; it's an ongoing process. By assessing risks, defining objectives, and practicing your plan, you take control of your home's safety. In the next chapter, we'll dive into the details of conducting a thorough security audit to identify and address vulnerabilities.

Preparation isn't a one-time effort; it's an ongoing process. By assessing risks, defining objectives, and practicing your plan, you take control of your home's safety. These steps transform your house into a fortress—a place where you and your family can feel secure no matter what happens. In the next chapter, we'll dive into the details of conducting a thorough security audit to identify and address vulnerabilities.

Chapter 3: Conducting a Security Audit

Finding the Weak Spots

Every fortress has its vulnerabilities, and your home is no exception. Even the most well-protected spaces can have weak points that go unnoticed until it's too late. Conducting a comprehensive security audit of your property is essential to identifying these vulnerabilities and addressing them proactively. This chapter will guide you through a detailed, step-by-step process to evaluate your home's defenses, with actionable advice to fortify every aspect of your living space.

Imagine your home from the perspective of an intruder. What would they see? What areas look easy to breach, and what might deter them? By thinking like a potential threat, you can uncover weaknesses and transform your home into a stronghold.

Understanding the Threat Landscape

Before diving into the specifics of your home's vulnerabilities, it's critical to understand the broader landscape of threats that may target your household. Different environments, lifestyles, and societal factors shape the risks you face. For instance:

- **Urban Areas:** Higher population density often correlates with increased crime rates, making theft and vandalism common concerns.
- **Rural Settings:** Remote locations may face delayed law enforcement response times and wildlife hazards, but they're less likely to experience opportunistic break-ins.
- **Weather-Related Risks:** Tornadoes, hurricanes, or wildfires can expose structural vulnerabilities that criminals could later exploit.

Analyzing these broader factors allows you to tailor your audit and address risks effectively. Combine this understanding with localized knowledge of your neighborhood and property to form a comprehensive approach.

Finding the Weak Spots in Everyday Activities

Many vulnerabilities arise not from structural issues but from daily habits and routines. These unnoticed patterns can provide critical insights to a potential intruder. Consider the following examples:

- **Predictable Schedules:** Leaving and returning home at the same time every day makes it easier for someone to anticipate when your house will be unoccupied.
- **Open Garage Doors:** Frequently left open while performing yard work or unloading groceries, this area is a weak point often overlooked.

- **Unsecured Packages:** Deliveries left on your porch can indicate whether you're home or away, providing clues to an observer.

Pro Tip: Incorporate unpredictability into your routines. Adjust your daily schedule occasionally, or use timers for lights and electronics to give the illusion of activity when you're away.

Step 1: Start at the Perimeter

The first line of defense for any home is its perimeter. This includes the boundary of your property, such as fences, gates, landscaping, and lighting. Here's how to conduct a thorough inspection:

- **Fencing and Gates:**
    - Inspect for gaps, weak points, or areas where the fence could be climbed. Chain-link fences and metal fencing offer better security than wood, which can be cut or burned.
    - Ensure gates are equipped with heavy-duty locks and reinforced hinges. A sagging gate is an easy target for forced entry.
- **Lighting:**
    - Walk around your property at night. Are there areas of complete darkness? Motion-activated floodlights are ideal for illuminating potential hiding spots.
    - Consider solar-powered options for hard-to-reach areas to ensure consistent lighting without running up electricity bills.
- **Landscaping:**
    - Trim overgrown shrubs and trees that provide cover for intruders. Keep bushes near windows below waist height.
    - Install thorny plants like rose bushes beneath windows as a natural deterrent.

Perimeter Vulnerability Checklist	Action
Motion-activated lights installed?	Yes/No
Shrubs and trees trimmed?	Yes/No
Fencing/gates inspected?	Yes/No

Real-Life Example:

A homeowner I worked with had a dense hedge along their backyard fence, which provided cover for potential intruders. By trimming the hedge and adding motion-activated lights, they transformed a blind spot into a deterrent.

Step 2: Entry Point Inspection

Doors, windows, and other access points are the most common targets for break-ins. A strong perimeter means little if your entry points are easy to breach.

- **Doors:**
    - Ensure all exterior doors are solid-core or reinforced steel. Hollow-core doors can be kicked in easily.
    - Install deadbolts with at least a one-inch throw, and reinforce the strike plate with 3-inch screws that anchor into the wall frame.
    - Consider adding door reinforcement bars or door jammers for extra security.
- **Windows:**
    - Fit windows with secure locks and consider adding shatter-resistant film to prevent glass from breaking easily.
    - For sliding windows, place a wooden or metal rod in the track to prevent them from being forced open.
- **Garage Doors:**
    - Inspect the garage door's locking mechanism and consider upgrading to one with a manual override that can't be easily accessed from outside.
    - Ensure the door between the garage and the house is as secure as your exterior doors.

Entry Point Security Checklist	Action Required
Motion-activated floodlights	Yes/No
Window locks secure?	Yes/No
Shatter-resistant film applied?	Yes/No
Garage door locks upgraded?	Yes/No

Pro Tip: A reinforced front door can withstand up to 1,000 pounds of force. It's worth the investment.

Step 3: Interior Security

If an intruder breaches your perimeter and entry points, your home's interior becomes your last line of defense. Strengthen it to protect your family and valuables.

- **Safe Rooms:**
    - Designate a secure room with a solid-core door, a heavy-duty lock, and a reinforced frame. Stock it with essential supplies, such as water, first aid kits, and communication tools like a charged cell phone or two-way radio.
- **Alarms and Sensors:**
    - Install a monitored alarm system with sensors on all doors and windows. Glass-break detectors can add an extra layer of protection.
- **Surveillance Cameras:**
    - Position cameras to cover key areas like entryways, hallways, and staircases. Opt for systems that allow remote access via smartphone apps.

Interior Defense Features	Purpose
Safe room created?	Yes/No
Monitored alarm system installed?	Yes/No
Cameras positioned strategically?	Yes/No

Step 4: Simulate and Test Your Defenses

A security audit isn't complete without testing. Simulating real-life scenarios helps identify weak points and improve your response.

- **Mock Break-Ins:** Ask a friend or family member to simulate attempting entry while you assess vulnerabilities.
- **Emergency Drills:** Practice what to do if an intruder is detected. Include steps like locking doors, gathering in a safe room, and contacting authorities.
- **Regular Reviews:** Repeat your audit at least once a year or after significant changes, such as renovations or new technology installations.

Real-Life SEAL Insight: Layered Defense Saves Lives

During one mission, my team secured a compound with multiple defense layers: external barriers, reinforced entry points, and secure rooms inside. When a breach occurred, these layers slowed the attackers and gave us time to respond. The same principle applies to your home—every layer buys you critical seconds in an emergency.

Conducting a security audit isn't about creating a fortress of paranoia. It's about empowering yourself with knowledge and taking proactive steps to protect your family. In the next chapter, we'll discuss how to build layered defenses that work together to deter and neutralize threats.

Taking Your Security Further

- **Technology Integration:**
    - Smart home devices like video doorbells, automated locks, and motion sensors can enhance your security system. Ensure all devices are encrypted to prevent cyber intrusions.
- **Neighborhood Collaboration:**
    - Coordinate with neighbors to create a watch system. Sharing information about suspicious activity can benefit everyone.
- **Fortify Weak Points:**

- If you identify recurring vulnerabilities, invest in higher-grade materials or professional security consultations.

Conducting a security audit isn't about creating a fortress of paranoia—it's about empowering yourself with knowledge and taking proactive steps to protect your family. By regularly inspecting your perimeter, securing entry points, and strengthening interior defenses, you're building a layered approach to safety. In the next chapter, we'll delve deeper into creating multi-layered defense systems that work together seamlessly to deter, delay, and neutralize potential threats.

Chapter 4: Layers of Defense

Building a Multi-Layered Defense System

A single lock on your front door won't stop a determined intruder. True home defense relies on multiple layers of protection, each designed to deter, delay, and neutralize threats before they reach you and your family. In this chapter, we'll explore how to create a robust, layered defense system, starting from your property's perimeter and moving inward to the heart of your home.

A layered defense is not just about physical barriers but also about psychological deterrence, smart technology, and strategic preparation. Each layer strengthens the one before it, creating a comprehensive system that ensures your home is as secure as possible.

Why Layers Matter: The Defense-in-Depth Principle

In SEAL operations, layered defense strategies are critical to mission success. Each layer—from early detection to final fortifications—is designed to slow attackers and give defenders the upper hand. Applying this principle to your home ensures that no single failure leaves you exposed. Every layer buys time, increases complexity for intruders, and enhances your family's safety.

Imagine an intruder navigating your defenses. They encounter a locked gate, a well-lit yard, and a thorny hedge. If they press forward, they find reinforced doors, shatter-resistant windows, and a loud alarm system. Each of these obstacles raises the effort and risk required to gain entry, making your home less attractive as a target.

The Role of Deterrence

Deterrence is the first goal of any defense system. The harder your home looks to breach, the less likely an intruder is to attempt entry. Criminals often choose targets based on perceived vulnerability, so making your property look uninviting can prevent a break-in before it begins.

- **Visual Cues:** A well-maintained property with visible security measures signals that the home is occupied and protected.
- **Unpredictable Activity:** Use timers for lights and electronics to simulate occupancy when you're away.
- **Auditory Deterrents:** Dogs, whether small and loud or large and intimidating, act as natural deterrents by alerting owners to strangers.

Real-Life Example: A homeowner in a high-crime area installed fake cameras alongside real ones, positioned prominently around their property. Coupled with security signage and regular yard maintenance, they saw a significant drop in suspicious activity on their street.

Layered Defense Beyond the Physical

While physical barriers are essential, a truly effective defense system integrates psychological, technological, and procedural elements. This multi-dimensional approach ensures that even if one layer is bypassed, others remain intact to mitigate the risk.

Psychological Elements:

- Visible signs of security systems and surveillance create the impression of constant monitoring.
- Regular activity around the home, such as outdoor chores or visible neighbors, increases perceived risk for potential intruders.

Technological Enhancements:

- Modern smart home systems allow remote monitoring and control of locks, lights, and cameras.
- Smartphone alerts can notify you instantly of unusual activity, whether you're home or away.

Procedural Measures:

- Family routines, such as locking all doors by a certain time each night, form an integral part of your defense system.
- Emergency drills ensure every family member knows their role during a break-in or other crisis.

Pro Tip: Even low-cost measures, like adding window decals or installing inexpensive motion sensors, contribute to a multi-layered defense system without breaking the bank.

The Importance of Redundancy

In the SEALs, redundancy is a cornerstone of safety and preparedness. This concept applies equally to home defense. If one layer of security fails, another layer should immediately engage to slow or stop the threat. Redundancy might include:

- Backup lighting systems (e.g., solar-powered or battery-operated lights in case of a power outage).
- Secondary locks on windows and doors.
- Multiple communication devices, such as a landline, mobile phone, and walkie-talkies, to ensure connectivity during emergencies.

Real-Life Example: During a neighborhood blackout, a family's solar-powered motion lights and battery-operated alarms provided continuous protection, deterring opportunistic burglars who targeted nearby homes left in darkness.

Thinking Like an Intruder

To identify weaknesses in your defense, imagine approaching your home as a potential intruder. Consider:

1. **What would draw attention to this property as a target?**
   - Are there areas with poor visibility or easy access points?
   - Does the home appear unoccupied or poorly maintained?
2. **What obstacles would deter entry?**
   - Are there visible barriers, such as fences, gates, and hedges?
   - Are security cameras or signs prominently displayed?
3. **How long would it take to bypass the defenses?**
   - Are doors and windows reinforced?
   - Are there audible alarms or motion-activated lights that could alert neighbors or the authorities?

Pro Tip: Conduct regular walk-throughs of your property during the day and night. Pay attention to shadowy areas, blind spots, and places where visibility is limited.

By understanding the principles of layered defense and implementing them methodically, you can create a home that is not only physically secure but also psychologically unappealing to intruders. These layers work together seamlessly to deter, delay, and neutralize threats, ensuring that your family is protected at every stage.

Layer 1: Perimeter Defense

The perimeter of your property serves as the first line of defense. A strong perimeter discourages intruders from approaching your home in the first place.

- **Fencing and Barriers:**
  - Install durable fencing that is difficult to climb or cut. Options like wrought iron or chain-link are both secure and visually deterrent.
  - Use landscaping strategically. Thorny plants such as roses or barberry bushes can create natural barriers around vulnerable areas like windows or fences.
- **Gates and Driveways:**
  - Equip gates with heavy-duty locks and consider adding an intercom system for visitor screening.
  - For driveways, consider installing a secure gate or using automatic bollards to control vehicle access.
- **Lighting:**
  - Use motion-activated floodlights to illuminate dark corners and entry points. Intruders are less likely to approach a well-lit property.
  - Solar-powered lights along pathways and around fences provide continuous illumination without relying on the grid.

Perimeter Defense Features	Effectiveness	Cost
Motion-activated floodlights	High	Moderate
Chain link or metal fencing	Medium to High	High
Security system signage	Medium	Low

Real-Life Example:

One homeowner installed motion-activated floodlights and signage after a string of burglaries in their area. The added visibility and psychological deterrents reduced attempted break-ins in their neighborhood.

Layer 2: Entry Point Reinforcement

Doors and windows are the most common targets for intruders. Reinforcing these access points is critical to delaying or deterring entry.

- **Doors:**
    - Use solid-core or steel doors for all exterior entry points. Hollow-core doors can be kicked in with minimal effort.
    - Install deadbolts with a one-inch throw and reinforce strike plates with 3-inch screws.
    - Consider door reinforcement kits, which include metal plates and bars to strengthen the door frame.
- **Windows:**
    - Apply shatter-resistant film or security laminate to all ground-level windows.
    - Install window locks or pins to prevent them from being pried open.
    - Use window bars for areas with higher crime rates, ensuring they are equipped with emergency release mechanisms for safety.
- **Garage Doors:**
    - Secure your garage door with a manual lock or reinforced locking bar.
    - Install an automatic garage door closer to prevent it from being left open inadvertently.

Pro Tip: A door with a reinforced frame can withstand up to 1,000 pounds of force, significantly slowing down an intruder and buying you critical time.

Entry Point Security Features	Purpose	Recommendation
Solid-core doors	Strengthen entryways	Front and back doors
Shatter-resistant window film	Prevent window breakage	Ground floor and basement
Garage door locks	Secure a common entry point	Interior and exterior locks

Layer 3: Interior Defense

If an intruder manages to breach your perimeter and entry points, your home's interior becomes the final line of defense.

- **Safe Rooms:**
    - Designate a secure room equipped with a reinforced door, heavy-duty lock, and communication tools like a charged cell phone or two-way radio.
    - Stock the safe room with water, non-perishable food, first aid supplies, and an emergency flashlight.
- **Alarm Systems:**
    - Install a monitored alarm system that triggers an alert if an entry point is breached. Choose a system with cellular backup to function during power outages.
    - Add motion sensors in hallways and main living areas to detect unauthorized movement.
- **Surveillance Cameras:**
    - Use cameras with remote monitoring capabilities to keep an eye on your home even when you're away.
    - Place cameras in high-traffic areas like hallways, entry points, and staircases.

Interior Defense Features	Purpose	Placement
Safe room	Family protection in crises	Central location
Alarm system	Alert and deter intruders	Whole house
Pepper spray	Immediate defense	Accessible areas

Layer 4: Psychological Deterrence

A well-protected home sends a clear message to potential intruders: "This house isn't worth the risk." Psychological deterrence can be as powerful as physical barriers.

- **Visible Security Features:**
    - Display security system signage prominently. Even if you don't have a system, signs alone can deter opportunistic criminals.
    - Use fake cameras in addition to real ones to increase the perceived level of surveillance.
- **Dogs:**
    - Even small dogs can act as effective deterrents by barking at strangers. Larger breeds trained for protection add another layer of security.
- **Behavioral Tactics:**
    - Use timers to turn lights and TVs on and off when you're away, creating the illusion of occupancy.
    - Maintain a tidy yard and driveway. An overgrown yard or piled-up mail signals that a house may be unoccupied.

Chapter 5: Defensive Tools and Gear

Tools That Make the Difference

Even the best defense plans are incomplete without the right tools and equipment to execute them. From high-tech surveillance to everyday items that can double as defensive tools, this chapter provides a detailed guide to selecting, using, and maintaining the gear you need to keep your home secure. By combining advanced technology with practical solutions, you can create a well-equipped, adaptable system that protects your family in any scenario.

Beyond the Basics: The Philosophy of Gear Selection

Choosing the right defensive tools isn't just about picking the most expensive or high-tech items on the market. It's about understanding your unique needs, the threats you're most likely to face, and how each piece of equipment fits into your overall defense strategy. Tools should complement your environment, your skill level, and your family's capabilities, creating a cohesive system that works seamlessly under pressure.

- **Adaptability Matters:** Tools that serve multiple purposes are invaluable. For example, a high-lumen flashlight can illuminate dark areas, act as a signaling device, and temporarily blind an attacker.
- **Simplicity Over Complexity:** In high-stress situations, complex gadgets can become liabilities. Opt for tools that are intuitive to use, even under duress.
- **Reliability is Key:** The most effective tools are those that work flawlessly when needed. Invest in equipment with a reputation for durability and performance.

Real-Life Insight: During a training mission, my team once relied on a single multi-tool to perform tasks ranging from cutting through obstacles to making minor repairs. This reinforced the importance of having versatile, dependable gear.

Integrating Tools with Your Environment

Every home is different, and your choice of tools should reflect your specific layout and surroundings. Begin by analyzing your property and identifying areas where tools can provide the greatest advantage:

- **Entry Points:** Ensure you have tools like door braces or reinforced locks for all doors and windows. Sliding doors, in particular, benefit from additional security measures like track bars.

- **High-Traffic Areas:** Install motion-activated cameras or alarms in areas where intruders are most likely to pass, such as hallways, staircases, or driveways.
- **Blind Spots:** Address areas that are out of sight from the main living spaces. Tools like wide-angle surveillance cameras or mirrors can help eliminate these vulnerabilities.

Pro Tip: Conduct a walk-through of your home during both day and night. Pay attention to how lighting and shadows affect visibility, and plan your tool placement accordingly.

Psychological Power of Visible Tools

Some tools are as much about deterring intruders as they are about actively defending your home. Visible security measures send a clear message that your property is protected and prepared.

- **Security Signage:** Even if you're using affordable, DIY security systems, prominently displaying signs can deter opportunistic criminals.
- **Decoy Cameras:** Install fake cameras in addition to functional ones to amplify the appearance of surveillance.
- **Strategic Lighting:** Motion-activated lights not only illuminate your property but also startle would-be intruders, making them reconsider their plans.

Real-Life Example: A family in a suburban neighborhood installed dummy cameras alongside real ones and paired them with motion-activated floodlights. This simple, cost-effective setup drastically reduced loitering and suspicious activity near their property.

The Role of Training in Effective Tool Use

A defensive tool is only as effective as the person using it. Training and familiarity are critical to ensuring that you can deploy your gear confidently and correctly when it matters most.

1. Skill Development:

- Practice using tools like pepper spray, tasers, or flashlights in realistic scenarios. Understand their range, limitations, and ideal deployment techniques.
- Schedule regular drills to rehearse how to respond to various threats. Include all family members in these sessions to ensure everyone knows their role.

2. Maintenance Routine:

- Inspect all tools periodically to confirm they're in working condition. Replace expired items like pepper spray or first aid supplies promptly.
- Keep batteries charged and test electronic devices like cameras, alarms, and flashlights monthly.

3. Realistic Expectations:

- Understand that tools are part of a larger strategy. For example, a taser may incapacitate an intruder temporarily, but it's not a standalone solution. Combine it with an alarm system or safe room protocols for comprehensive protection.

Pro Tip: Practice deploying tools under simulated stress conditions. This helps build muscle memory and ensures you remain calm and effective in real emergencies.

Budgeting for Your Defense System

Home defense doesn't have to break the bank. By prioritizing essential tools and spreading investments over time, you can build a robust system without unnecessary financial strain.

- **Start Small:** Focus on high-impact, low-cost items like door braces, window locks, and motion-activated lights.
- **Plan Upgrades:** Gradually add advanced tools like surveillance cameras, smart locks, or non-lethal weapons as your budget allows.
- **DIY Options:** Many effective solutions, such as installing security film on windows or creating a hidden safe, can be accomplished with minimal expense and basic tools.

Sample Budget Allocation:

Category	Percentage	Example Tools
Entry Point Security	40%	Door braces, deadbolts
Surveillance and Alarms	30%	Cameras, motion sensors
Non-Lethal Defensive Tools	20%	Pepper spray, stun guns
Miscellaneous Items	10%	Batteries, signage

Integrating Smart Technology

The rise of smart home technology has revolutionized defensive tools, offering unprecedented convenience and control. Integrating these systems into your overall defense plan can amplify their effectiveness.

- **Remote Monitoring:** Modern cameras and alarms allow you to check on your property from anywhere using a smartphone app.
- **Automated Alerts:** Receive instant notifications when motion is detected, a door is unlocked, or an alarm is triggered.
- **Customization:** Program smart devices to activate in specific scenarios. For instance, schedule outdoor lights to turn on automatically when motion is detected after dark.

Real-Life Insight: One homeowner paired a smart doorbell with motion sensors and automated lighting. When someone approached the front door, the system activated both a spotlight and a camera, capturing the intruder's face and scaring them away simultaneously.

By understanding the full spectrum of defensive tools and integrating them into a cohesive plan, you can create a home that is not only physically secure but also psychologically unappealing to intruders. Remember, the key is to balance technology, practicality, and training to ensure every tool is used to its fullest potential.

Category 1: Non-Lethal Defensive Tools

Non-lethal tools are effective for deterring intruders without escalating to lethal force.

- **Pepper Spray:** Compact and easy to use, pepper spray is highly effective at immobilizing attackers temporarily.
- **Tasers:** Offer a strong deterrent and incapacitate intruders from a distance.
- **Personal Alarms:** Loud alarms can disorient intruders and alert neighbors.

Tool	Range	Ease of Use	Effectiveness	Cost
Pepper Spray	Short	High	Medium	Low
Taser	Medium	Moderate	High	High
Personal Alarm	Audible Area	Very High	Low to Medium	Low to Medium

Category 2: Tactical Tools for Home Defense

Tactical tools provide more robust defensive capabilities but require training to use effectively.

- **Flashlights:** High-lumen flashlights can temporarily blind attackers and are essential in low-light conditions.
- **Baton or Club:** Useful for close-range defense; lightweight and easy to store.
- **Firearms (if legally owned):** Provide a last-resort option for defending your home. Always secure firearms properly in locked safes or storage areas.

Category 3: Defensive Infrastructure

Enhance your home's security with strategically placed gear.

- **Surveillance Cameras:** Install cameras at entry points and high-risk areas.
- **Door Braces:** Simple devices that add significant resistance to forced entry.
- **Window Bars or Films:** Reinforce windows to prevent breakage or unauthorized access.

Pie Chart: Budget Allocation for Defensive Infrastructure

A chart dividing a typical budget into categories like surveillance (40%), window reinforcement (30%), and door bracing (30%).

Training and Maintenance

Even the best tools are useless without proper training and upkeep.

- **Practice:** Learn how to use your tools effectively. For instance, practice deploying pepper spray or using a flashlight tactically.
- **Regular Inspections:** Check batteries, expiration dates, and functionality of all devices.
- **Family Drills:** Ensure every family member knows how and when to use the tools at their disposal.

Real-Life SEAL Insight: Gear Is Secondary to Skill

In SEAL training, we learned that tools are only as effective as the person using them. The best gear in the world won't save you if you don't know how to use it. Invest in training, not just equipment.

Equipping Your Fortress

Even the best defense plans are incomplete without the right tools and equipment to execute them. From high-tech surveillance to everyday items that can double as defensive tools, this chapter provides a detailed guide to selecting, using, and maintaining the gear you need to keep your home secure. By combining advanced technology with practical solutions, you can create a well-equipped, adaptable system that protects your family in any scenario.

Step 1: Choosing the Right Surveillance Systems

A robust surveillance system is a cornerstone of modern home defense. Cameras do more than just record—they deter intruders, provide critical evidence, and help you monitor activity in and around your home.

- **Step 1.1: Assess Your Surveillance Needs**
  - Identify key areas to monitor, such as entry points (front and back doors), driveways, and blind spots around the property.
  - Consider indoor cameras for high-traffic areas or rooms with valuables.
- **Step 1.2: Select the Right Cameras**
  - **Wired vs. Wireless:** Wired systems are more reliable but require professional installation. Wireless cameras are easier to set up and can be repositioned.
  - **Resolution:** Choose cameras with at least 1080p resolution for clear video.

- **Night Vision:** Ensure your cameras have infrared or low-light capabilities to monitor activity after dark.
- **Smart Features:** Look for motion detection, facial recognition, and smartphone integration.
- **Step 1.3: Installation Tips**
  - Mount cameras at a height of 8-10 feet to reduce tampering and maximize visibility.
  - Angle cameras to cover key areas without blind spots. Use overlapping fields of view for critical zones.

Pro Tip: Combine visible cameras with hidden ones. Visible cameras deter intruders, while hidden cameras capture unguarded actions.

Step 2: Enhancing Entry Point Security

Your doors and windows are the most vulnerable parts of your home. Reinforcing these entry points is crucial for keeping intruders out.

- **Step 2.1: Door Reinforcements**
  - Replace hollow-core doors with solid-core or steel options. These can withstand greater force.
  - Install deadbolt locks with a one-inch throw and ensure the strike plate is secured with 3-inch screws that anchor into the wall frame.
  - Add door reinforcement bars or jammers for an extra layer of protection.
  - Use peepholes or smart doorbells to identify visitors without opening the door.

Detailed Example: Imagine an intruder attempting to kick in your front door. A standard hollow-core door would likely break after a few attempts. However, a solid-core door reinforced with a steel plate and a deadbolt will resist repeated force, delaying the intruder and potentially causing them to abandon their attempt altogether.

- **Step 2.2: Window Security**
  - Apply shatter-resistant film to windows to prevent glass from breaking easily.
  - Install window locks and consider adding window bars for ground-level windows. Ensure bars have quick-release mechanisms for emergency egress.
  - Use security sensors that trigger an alarm when windows are opened or broken.

Pro Tip: Don't overlook sliding doors. Use security bars or pins to prevent them from being forced open.

Step 3: Leveraging Technology for Alerts and Automation

Smart home technology has revolutionized home defense, making it easier to monitor and control your security systems remotely.

- **Step 3.1: Alarm Systems**
  - Choose monitored alarm systems that notify a security company or local authorities when triggered.
  - Install sensors on all entry points and add motion detectors for critical areas.

- **Step 3.2: Smart Locks**
    - Replace traditional locks with smart locks that allow keyless entry via PIN codes, smartphone apps, or biometric scans.
    - Set temporary codes for guests or service providers, and monitor lock activity remotely.
- **Step 3.3: Lighting Automation**
    - Use smart lighting systems to create the illusion of occupancy when you're away. Schedule lights to turn on and off at random intervals.
    - Pair motion-activated lights with cameras for enhanced surveillance.

Detailed Example: A homeowner installed a smart lighting system that turned on specific lights when their camera detected motion. This startled a would-be intruder who fled as soon as the lights activated, showing how automation can enhance security.

Step 4: Non-Lethal Defensive Tools

In situations where physical confrontation is unavoidable, non-lethal tools provide effective ways to incapacitate intruders without causing permanent harm.

- **Step 4.1: Pepper Spray**
    - Compact and easy to use, pepper spray temporarily blinds and incapacitates attackers.
    - Keep it in accessible locations, like near entry points or in your safe room.
- **Step 4.2: Stun Guns and Tasers**
    - These devices deliver an electric shock to incapacitate an attacker. Choose models with a safety switch to prevent accidental discharge.
- **Step 4.3: Personal Alarms**
    - Small, battery-operated devices emit a loud noise when activated, drawing attention and scaring off intruders.

Pro Tip: Train your family members on how to use non-lethal tools safely and effectively.

Step 5: Emergency Supplies for Crises

Preparing for emergencies means having the right tools and supplies on hand to sustain your family during disruptions.

- **Step 5.1: Backup Power Sources**
    - Invest in a generator or solar power system to keep essential devices running during outages.
    - Store fuel safely and rotate it regularly to maintain its usability.
- **Step 5.2: Fire Safety Equipment**
    - Install fire extinguishers in key areas like the kitchen and garage. Learn how to use them properly.
    - Add smoke detectors and carbon monoxide alarms, checking batteries regularly.
- **Step 5.3: First Aid Kits**
    - Stock comprehensive first aid kits with bandages, antiseptics, pain relievers, and medical tools. Ensure it includes supplies for specific family needs, like prescription medications.

Pro Tip: Organize emergency supplies in easy-to-carry bags in case of evacuation.

Step 6: Regular Maintenance and Training

The most advanced tools are useless if they aren't maintained or if you don't know how to use them.

- **Step 6.1: Maintenance Checklist**
    - Test alarm systems and cameras monthly to ensure they're functioning properly.
    - Replace batteries in smoke detectors and sensors regularly.
    - Clean camera lenses and ensure firmware is up to date.
- **Step 6.2: Family Training**
    - Conduct regular drills to practice using tools and responding to emergencies.
    - Familiarize every family member with the location and operation of key devices, such as fire extinguishers and first aid kits.

Real-Life SEAL Insight

In the field, my team relied on regular checks of our gear and constant training to ensure readiness. At home, the same principles apply. A well-maintained system and a trained household can handle crises more effectively than the most advanced equipment left untested.

Chapter 6: Stockpiling Essentials Navy SEAL Style

Be Ready for Anything

When disaster strikes, the first things to disappear are often the ones we take for granted—clean water, food, and medical supplies. Having a well-stocked and thoughtfully prepared inventory can mean the difference between survival and desperation. This chapter will teach you how to assemble a practical, efficient, and discreet stockpile based on lessons learned in the field.

Why Stockpiling Matters

Stockpiling isn't just about preparing for rare, catastrophic events like hurricanes or earthquakes. Everyday disruptions, such as power outages, supply chain delays, or even unexpected illness, can leave you scrambling for essentials. A well-planned stockpile ensures that you're ready for any scenario—from minor inconveniences to major crises. It's not about hoarding; it's about being smart, efficient, and prepared.

Imagine this: a sudden winter storm hits your area, and roads become impassable. Grocery stores are stripped of essentials within hours. Without a stockpile, you're left to ration whatever you happen to have on hand. But with a well-organized supply, you can ride out the storm comfortably, knowing your family's needs are covered. This peace of mind is the ultimate goal of stockpiling.

Stockpiling vs. Hoarding: The Key Differences

While the media often portrays stockpiling negatively, there's a critical distinction between preparedness and hoarding. Hoarding is reactive, driven by panic, and often leads to waste and inefficiency. Stockpiling, on the other hand, is proactive, methodical, and focused on sustainability. Here are some key differences:

- **Purpose:** Stockpiling is about ensuring your family's safety and comfort. Hoarding often stems from fear and lacks a clear plan.
- **Organization:** A stockpile is carefully planned, regularly rotated, and tailored to specific needs. Hoarding results in clutter and disorganization.
- **Impact:** Stockpiling considers the needs of the broader community, while hoarding contributes to shortages and disrupts supply chains.

Pro Tip: When building your stockpile, focus on quality over quantity. A small, well-organized supply is far more effective than piles of random items that don't meet your needs.

Psychological Benefits of Being Prepared

Beyond the tangible advantages, stockpiling provides significant psychological benefits. Knowing that you're prepared for emergencies reduces stress and anxiety, allowing you to focus on what truly matters: keeping your family safe. This sense of control is invaluable during chaotic situations.

Real-Life Insight: A friend of mine in the SEALs once described the mental clarity he felt during a deployment because he knew his gear and supplies were squared away. "Preparation clears your mind," he said. The same principle applies at home. A well-stocked supply gives you one less thing to worry about when crises arise.

Tailoring Your Stockpile to Your Family's Needs

No two households are the same, and your stockpile should reflect your unique circumstances. Consider the following factors:

- **Family Size:** A larger family requires more supplies, but efficiency is key. Bulk items like rice, beans, or powdered milk can stretch your stockpile further.
- **Dietary Restrictions:** If someone in your household has allergies, dietary restrictions, or preferences, ensure your stockpile accommodates these needs.
- **Age Range:** Young children and elderly family members may require specialized items, such as baby formula, diapers, or medications.
- **Pets:** Don't forget about your furry friends! Stock up on pet food, litter, and any necessary medications.

Pro Tip: Create a checklist for each family member, listing their specific needs. Use this as a guide when shopping and organizing your supplies.

Planning for Long-Term Emergencies

While most emergencies are short-term, it's wise to prepare for scenarios where supplies might be needed for weeks or even months. Long-term preparedness involves:

1. **Diversified Food Storage:** Include a mix of shelf-stable items (e.g., canned goods, freeze-dried meals) and foods with extended shelf lives, like grains and legumes stored in vacuum-sealed containers.
2. **Water Independence:** Beyond storing bottled water, invest in purification tools such as filters or rainwater collection systems (where legal).
3. **Energy Solutions:** Stockpile batteries, solar chargers, or a small generator to maintain power during extended outages.

Real-Life Example: During the Texas freeze of 2021, families with access to backup generators and alternative water sources were able to maintain basic living conditions, while others struggled without heat or clean water.

Integrating Stockpiling Into Daily Life

One common mistake is treating stockpiles as separate from everyday life. Instead, make your stockpile part of your regular routine:

- **Rotational Use:** Use items from your stockpile in your daily meals and replace them during regular shopping trips. This prevents waste and ensures your supplies remain fresh.
- **Seasonal Adjustments:** Review your stockpile as seasons change. In winter, prioritize warmth and energy sources. In summer, focus on hydration and cooling methods.
- **Weekly Audits:** Spend a few minutes each week checking expiration dates and inventory levels. This simple habit keeps your stockpile ready for any situation.

Pro Tip: Keep a "grab-and-go" bag packed with essentials from your stockpile. This is especially useful for sudden evacuations, such as during wildfires or hurricanes.

Stockpiling as a Community Effort

Preparedness doesn't have to be a solo effort. Engaging with your community can enhance your stockpile's effectiveness and foster mutual support during emergencies:

- **Resource Sharing:** Coordinate with neighbors to pool resources. For example, one household might focus on medical supplies, while another stores bulk food items.
- **Neighborhood Drills:** Practice emergency scenarios as a group, such as evacuations or shelter-in-place protocols.
- **Shared Knowledge:** Exchange tips on stockpiling, storage, and resource management to build a collective knowledge base.

Real-Life Example: In a rural town affected by frequent flooding, neighbors created a shared stockpile of sandbags, water pumps, and non-perishable food. This collaborative effort saved time and resources during emergencies.

How to stockpile correctly
Step 1: Identify Your Needs

The first step in stockpiling is understanding your family's unique requirements. A successful stockpile isn't just about amassing supplies—it's about tailoring them to your specific circumstances.

- **Food and Water:** Calculate enough supplies to last for at least two weeks per person. This is your baseline. For longer emergencies, focus on items that are calorie-dense, shelf-stable, and easy to prepare.
    - **Food Examples:**
        - Canned goods (soups, vegetables, proteins like tuna or chicken).
        - Freeze-dried meals for long-term storage.
        - High-energy snacks like granola bars, trail mix, or protein bars.
    - **Water Examples:**

- Bottled water (14 gallons per person for two weeks).
- Water purification tablets or portable filters for emergencies.
- **Medical Supplies:** Tailor these to your family's health needs.
  - Basic first aid kit (bandages, antiseptic wipes, pain relievers).
  - Prescription medications (at least a 30-day supply if possible).
  - Supplies for chronic conditions (e.g., glucose monitors, asthma inhalers).
- **Other Essentials:**
  - Warmth: Blankets, hand warmers, and thermal clothing.
  - Communication Tools: Radios, phone chargers, and backup batteries.
  - Power Sources: Solar chargers, generators, or power banks.

Essential Stockpile Items by Category

Category	Examples	Quantity per Person (2 Weeks)
Food	Canned goods, freeze-dried meals	~14,000 calories
Water	Bottled water	14 gallons
Medical Supplies	First aid kit, medications	1 complete kit
Warmth	Blankets, hand warmers	2 per person
Communication Tools	Radios, phone chargers	1 set per family

Step 2: Efficient Storage Solutions

Space is often a limiting factor, but efficient storage techniques can help you maximize your stockpile without cluttering your living space.

- **Rotational Storage:** Organize supplies by expiration date. Place items with the earliest expiration dates in the front so they're used first. Replace consumed items during regular shopping trips.
- **Sealed Containers:** Store food and medical supplies in airtight, pest-resistant containers. For added protection, consider using vacuum-sealed bags for smaller items like grains or medications.
- **Hidden Storage:** Use creative storage solutions to keep critical supplies safe. For example:
  - Store canned goods under beds or in stackable bins.
  - Hide valuable items inside furniture with hollow compartments.
  - Use crawl spaces, attics, or false panels to conceal high-value supplies.

Pro Tip: Create a master list of your stockpile, noting quantities and expiration dates. This helps you track what you have and prevents over-purchasing.

Step 3: Tactical Tips for Stockpiling Food and Water

In the SEALs, resource management is a critical skill. The same principles apply to your stockpile, where conservation and smart planning are essential.

- **Food:**
  - Focus on calorie-dense options like peanut butter, nuts, and freeze-dried meals. These take up less space while providing essential energy.
  - Include a variety of foods to prevent "meal fatigue." Repeating the same meals can lower morale during prolonged crises.
- **Water:**
  - Store at least 1 gallon of water per person per day for drinking and basic hygiene.
  - Invest in water purification systems, such as portable filters or purification tablets, to extend your supply during prolonged crises.
  - Consider larger storage solutions, like rain barrels (where legal), for replenishing water supplies.

Method	Cost	Ease of Use	Effectiveness
Purification Tablets	Low	High	Medium
Portable Filters	Moderate	Moderate	High
Reverse Osmosis Unit	High	Low	Very High

Pro Tip: Always test purification methods before an emergency. Familiarity with tools like filters or tablets ensures you'll use them correctly when it matters most.

Step 4: Organize Your Stockpile

A cluttered and disorganized stockpile can create chaos during a crisis. Here's how to keep everything in order:

- **Categorize Supplies:** Group items into categories such as food, water, medical supplies, and tools. Use separate bins or shelves for each category.
- **Label Clearly:** Use waterproof labels to mark expiration dates, contents, and any special instructions (e.g., "Use water tablets after 30 minutes").
- **Spread It Out:** Avoid keeping all your supplies in one location. Diversify storage across multiple spots in your home to reduce the risk of losing everything in a single incident (e.g., fire or flooding).

Step 5: Protect Your Supplies

Your stockpile is only useful if it's safe from damage, theft, and contamination. Implement these measures to safeguard your inventory:

- **Temperature Control:** Store supplies in a cool, dry place to prevent spoilage. Avoid areas prone to extreme heat, like garages or attics.
- **Pest Prevention:** Use airtight containers to keep food safe from rodents and insects. Regularly inspect storage areas for signs of infestation.

- **Security:** Lock high-value items, such as backup power supplies and water filters, in a safe or secure room. Consider using combination locks for added protection.

Real-Life Example: During Hurricane Katrina, families who had stored water in sealed barrels and maintained a backup generator were able to ride out the storm for weeks, while others were left scrambling for basic necessities. Their foresight and preparation provided stability in an otherwise chaotic situation.

Step 6: Stockpile Maintenance

A neglected stockpile can be as dangerous as having no stockpile at all. Regular maintenance ensures your supplies are ready when you need them.

- **Regular Inspections:** Schedule monthly or quarterly checks to verify expiration dates, replace expired items, and ensure everything is in good condition.
- **Use and Replace:** Incorporate stockpile items into your daily life. This ensures rotation and prevents waste while keeping your stockpile fresh.
- **Family Involvement:** Teach everyone in your household where supplies are stored and how to use them. This reduces confusion during emergencies and ensures everyone is on the same page.

Real-Life SEAL Insight: Efficient Packing Saves Lives

When deployed, we carried only what we needed—but every item was carefully chosen and packed to maximize its usefulness. The same principle applies to your stockpile: it's not about having the most, but having the right things in the right quantities.

Stockpiling is not about hoarding; it's about being prepared. By building a practical, organized, and protected inventory, you ensure your family's survival and comfort during even the toughest situations. In the next chapter, we'll discuss energy independence and how to maintain power and utilities when traditional systems fail.

Chapter 7: Energy Independence

Staying Powered When the Grid Fails

Electricity powers nearly everything in our modern lives. From lighting and heating to communication and cooking, we rely on it without thinking. But what happens when the grid goes down? Whether it's due to a storm, a natural disaster, or infrastructure failure, losing power can quickly turn a manageable situation into a crisis. In this chapter, we'll explore how to achieve energy independence, ensuring you can maintain essential functions no matter what happens.

Why Energy Independence Is Essential

The modern world is built on a fragile infrastructure of centralized power. Most households depend entirely on the grid, leaving them vulnerable when it fails. Beyond natural disasters, grid failures can result from cyberattacks, energy shortages, or aging infrastructure. Being prepared with your own energy solutions transforms a moment of crisis into an opportunity for self-reliance and stability.

Imagine a scenario where a major storm leaves your neighborhood without power for weeks. Refrigerators stop working, communication lines are cut, and even simple tasks like cooking or staying warm become challenges. Energy independence not only ensures you can maintain these essentials but also provides peace of mind, allowing you to focus on keeping your family safe.

Understanding the Scope of Energy Needs

Many households underestimate how much energy they use daily. Preparing for grid failure begins with understanding what's truly essential and what can be reduced or eliminated during a crisis.

- **Critical Systems:** Appliances like refrigerators, heating and cooling units, and communication devices should be prioritized.
- **Convenience vs. Necessity:** During an outage, you'll need to distinguish between what's nice to have and what's essential for survival.
- **Energy Hierarchies:** Develop an energy priority list to allocate power effectively. For example, food preservation and lighting may take precedence over entertainment or convenience devices.

Real-Life Insight: During a prolonged outage, one family prioritized running their refrigerator and charging their phones. By turning off non-essential devices and using LED bulbs, they extended their generator's fuel supply by several days.

The Psychological Comfort of Energy Security

In high-stress situations, having access to reliable power provides more than just physical benefits. It can ease anxiety, maintain a sense of normalcy, and keep morale high. For families with children or elderly members, energy independence can mean the difference between a manageable disruption and a crisis.

- **Maintaining Communication:** Being able to charge phones or use radios ensures you can stay connected with loved ones and emergency services.
- **Lighting for Safety:** Darkness can exacerbate fear and uncertainty. Reliable lighting helps create a sense of security and control.
- **Preserving Comfort:** Simple things like powering a fan on a hot day or heating a small room in winter can significantly improve mental well-being during a prolonged outage.

Pro Tip: Create a designated "powered zone" in your home where critical devices and comfort items are prioritized. This helps your family stay organized and focused during outages.

Balancing Renewable and Non-Renewable Options

Energy independence involves using a mix of renewable and non-renewable sources. Each option has its strengths and limitations, and combining them ensures a reliable energy supply under varying conditions.

- **Renewables:** Solar panels and wind turbines offer long-term sustainability but depend on weather conditions.
- **Non-Renewables:** Generators powered by gasoline, propane, or diesel provide immediate energy but require ongoing fuel supplies.
- **Hybrid Systems:** Combining renewables with backup generators or battery banks maximizes reliability and efficiency.

Real-Life Example: A homeowner installed solar panels to power their daily energy needs while relying on a propane generator for backup during cloudy days. This hybrid approach provided consistent energy regardless of weather or grid conditions.

Planning for Long-Term Outages

Short-term outages lasting a few hours or days are inconvenient, but long-term outages demand a more comprehensive strategy. Planning for extended grid failures involves:

1. **Scalability:** Ensure your energy system can be expanded over time. Start with basic solar panels or a small generator and add capacity as your budget allows.
2. **Redundancy:** Have multiple energy sources to reduce reliance on a single system. For example, pair solar panels with a generator or battery backup.
3. **Sustainability:** Focus on renewable energy solutions like solar or wind for prolonged independence. These options reduce your dependence on fuel supplies.

Pro Tip: Keep detailed usage logs during short outages to identify gaps in your energy system. This helps you refine your setup for future emergencies.

Incorporating Energy Independence into Daily Life

Energy independence isn't just for emergencies. Integrating these systems into your daily routine improves efficiency, reduces costs, and ensures readiness.

- **Solar Power:** Use solar panels to offset your electricity bill and reduce reliance on the grid.
- **Battery Banks:** Charge batteries during peak sunlight hours and use them at night to save on energy costs.
- **Smart Energy Management:** Monitor energy usage with smart devices to identify areas where you can conserve power.

Real-Life Insight: A family in California reduced their energy bills by 30% by installing solar panels and shifting their appliance usage to daylight hours. During outages, their system seamlessly transitioned to off-grid mode.

The SEAL Mindset: Adapting and Overcoming

In the SEALs, adaptability is key to success. The same principle applies to energy independence. Equipment can fail, weather conditions can change, and unexpected challenges can arise. A flexible, problem-solving mindset ensures you're prepared for whatever comes your way.

- **Think Creatively:** Repurpose items to meet energy needs. For example, use camping stoves for cooking or hand-crank devices for small power needs.
- **Prepare for Worst-Case Scenarios:** Always have a backup plan for your backup plan. If your generator fails, do you have portable battery packs? If your solar panels are damaged, can you rely on stored fuel?

Pro Tip: Practice mock scenarios where you simulate a grid failure for 24-48 hours. This helps identify weaknesses in your system and improves your readiness.

How to secure electricity
Step 1: Understand Your Energy Needs

The first step to energy independence is knowing how much power you actually need. Start by identifying the essential appliances and devices your household relies on and calculating their daily energy requirements.

- **Lighting:** LED bulbs consume far less energy than traditional ones, making them ideal for emergencies. Switching to LEDs throughout your home can significantly reduce your overall power consumption.
- **Refrigeration:** A fridge or freezer is crucial for preserving perishable food, especially during prolonged outages.

- **Communication:** Devices like radios, phones, and laptops ensure you stay informed and connected with the outside world.
- **Heating and Cooling:** In extreme temperatures, systems like heaters or fans can be life-saving, especially for vulnerable family members like children or the elderly.

Appliance	Average Wattage	Daily Usage (Hours)	Daily Energy Needs (Wh)
LED Lighting (5 bulbs)	10 per bulb	6	300
Refrigerator	150	24	3,600
Smartphone Charger	5	4	20
Heater/Fan	100	8	800

Pro Tip: Keep a written list of your energy needs. During a crisis, this quick reference will help you prioritize which devices to power and when.

Step 2: Choose Your Power Sources

Once you understand your energy needs, you can explore options to generate and store power independently. Each source comes with its advantages and limitations, so selecting a combination of solutions can provide the most reliability.

- **Solar Panels:**
    - Install panels on your roof or in a sunny area of your property to harness sunlight. Solar panels are ideal for long-term energy independence.
    - Pair solar panels with a battery storage system to save excess energy for use at night or during cloudy weather.
- **Generators:**
    - Gas-powered generators are excellent for short-term needs but require proper fuel storage and regular maintenance.
    - Propane generators are quieter and emit fewer pollutants but may be less widely available.
- **Portable Power Stations:**
    - These battery-powered devices can charge small appliances and electronics during outages. They are portable and easy to use but have limited capacity.

Power Source	Pros	Cons
Solar Panels	Renewable, low maintenance costs	High initial investment
Generators	Reliable, easy to use	Requires fuel, noisy
Portable Power Stations	Portable, versatile	Limited capacity

Real-Life Example: A family in Florida invested in a hybrid system: rooftop solar panels with a battery bank for daytime use and a generator as backup for nighttime or stormy weather. This combination ensured they could maintain power even during extended outages.

Step 3: Store Energy Effectively

Power generation is only part of the equation; storage ensures you have energy when you need it most.

- **Battery Banks:**
    - Use lithium-ion or deep-cycle batteries to store power from solar panels or generators. These batteries are durable and can hold a charge for extended periods.
- **Fuel Storage:**
    - Store gasoline, diesel, or propane in approved containers in a well-ventilated area. Rotate fuel every 3-6 months to prevent degradation.
    - Consider fuel stabilizers to extend the shelf life of stored fuel.
- **Backup Systems:**
    - Keep smaller battery packs or power banks charged for critical devices like phones or flashlights. These are particularly useful for short-term outages.

Pro Tip: Invest in a battery management system to monitor charge levels and ensure efficient energy use.

Step 4: Optimize Energy Usage

When resources are limited, every watt counts. Being mindful of your energy consumption can extend your available power significantly.

- **Efficient Appliances:**
    - Invest in energy-efficient appliances, such as ENERGY STAR-certified refrigerators and heaters. These reduce overall consumption and maximize available power.
- **Time-Based Usage:**
    - Use high-demand devices like refrigerators during daylight hours when solar panels produce the most energy. Unplug devices that aren't in use to eliminate "phantom" power draw.
- **Zoning:**
    - Limit energy usage to specific areas of the home during outages. Focus on rooms where your family spends the most time.

Pro Tip: Use blackout curtains or thermal insulation to retain heat in the winter and cool air in the summer, reducing the need for energy-intensive HVAC systems.

Step 5: Water and Waste Systems

In addition to electricity, your home's water and waste systems may be compromised during a prolonged outage. Ensure you have contingencies in place to maintain hygiene and access to clean water.

- **Water Pumps:**
    - If you rely on a well, have a manual pump or a battery-powered backup to access water during a power outage.
- **Rainwater Collection:**
    - In areas where it's legal, set up rain barrels to collect water. Use filtration or purification tablets to make collected water safe for drinking.
- **Sanitation:**
    - Keep portable toilets or composting options as alternatives if plumbing becomes inoperable. Stock up on heavy-duty trash bags and disinfectants to manage waste.

Real-Life Example: A couple living in a rural area set up a rainwater collection system with filtration to supplement their water supply during a drought. When the grid failed for two weeks, they had clean water for drinking and basic hygiene.

Step 6: Maintain Your Systems

Energy independence requires ongoing care and preparation. Regular maintenance ensures your systems function when you need them most.

- **Solar Panels:**
    - Clean panels regularly to remove dust and debris that can reduce efficiency. Inspect wiring and connections for wear.
- **Generators:**
    - Run your generator periodically to ensure it's operational. Replace oil and filters as needed. Store fuel safely and replenish as required.
- **Batteries:**
    - Check for corrosion and ensure they are fully charged. Replace aging batteries before they fail.

Real-Life SEAL Insight: Redundancy Equals Resilience

In the field, we always had backups for our backups—redundant systems ensured we could operate under any conditions. The same principle applies to energy independence: don't rely on a single source or system.

Achieving energy independence isn't just about convenience; it's about ensuring you can weather any storm without losing control. In the next chapter, we'll shift our focus to medical preparedness, providing the tools and knowledge to handle health emergencies when professional help is unavailable.

Chapter 8: Medical Preparedness

When Every Second Counts

In an emergency, waiting for professional medical help might not be an option. Whether it's a natural disaster, a prolonged crisis, or a sudden injury, being prepared to handle medical emergencies can save lives. This chapter will guide you through building a professional-grade first aid kit, acquiring essential medical skills, and addressing common injuries and illnesses. Preparedness transforms fear and chaos into calm, controlled action—and that can make all the difference.

Why Medical Preparedness Is Critical

When emergencies strike, the first few minutes are often the most crucial. Quick, decisive action can mean the difference between life and death. Unfortunately, many people find themselves unprepared, relying solely on emergency responders who may be delayed during widespread crises. Medical preparedness empowers you to act decisively and effectively, ensuring the safety and well-being of your family when professional help isn't immediately available.

Consider this: In the aftermath of a hurricane, emergency services are often overwhelmed, roads may be impassable, and hospitals may be at capacity. In such situations, your ability to treat injuries, manage illnesses, and maintain hygiene becomes a cornerstone of survival. Medical preparedness isn't just about having supplies—it's about having the knowledge, skills, and confidence to use them.

The Psychological Impact of Being Prepared

Emergencies don't just affect physical health; they also take a toll on mental well-being. Fear, panic, and uncertainty can paralyze even the most capable individuals. Being medically prepared helps mitigate this psychological stress by giving you a sense of control. Knowing that you have the tools and skills to handle injuries or illnesses can significantly reduce anxiety and improve your decision-making during high-pressure situations.

Pro Tip: Keep a printed emergency medical guide alongside your first aid kit. This serves as a valuable reference during stressful moments, helping you stay calm and focused.

Tailoring Preparedness to Your Family's Needs

No two households are the same, and your medical preparedness plan should reflect your family's unique circumstances. Begin by assessing the following:

- **Age and Health:** Are there elderly family members, young children, or individuals with chronic conditions who may require specialized care?
- **Allergies and Sensitivities:** Ensure your kit includes medications and supplies tailored to known allergies or medical sensitivities.
- **Lifestyle and Activities:** Families who engage in outdoor activities, like hiking or camping, may need additional supplies for injuries like sprains or insect bites.
- **Pets:** Don't forget about your furry friends! Include pet-specific first aid items, such as wound care supplies and medications for common conditions.

Real-Life Insight: A family I worked with discovered during a preparedness review that their first aid kit lacked EpiPens for their child's severe peanut allergy. Adding this critical item ensured they were ready for a potential life-threatening reaction.

Integrating Medical Preparedness Into Daily Life

Medical preparedness isn't just for disasters. Integrating these practices into your daily life ensures you're always ready to respond to unexpected injuries or illnesses:

- **Regular Kit Checks:** Incorporate a monthly review of your first aid kit into your routine. Replace expired medications and replenish used supplies.
- **First Aid Drills:** Practice basic first aid techniques as a family. This helps build muscle memory and confidence in handling emergencies.
- **Everyday Use:** Use items from your first aid kit for minor injuries to ensure supplies are rotated and fresh.

Pro Tip: Keep a smaller version of your first aid kit in your car and another in your workplace. This ensures you're prepared no matter where an emergency occurs.

The Role of Community in Medical Preparedness

Medical preparedness isn't just an individual effort; it can also be a community endeavor. By coordinating with neighbors, schools, or local organizations, you can create a network of support that enhances everyone's safety.

- **Shared Resources:** Collaborate with neighbors to pool medical supplies and share knowledge. For example, one household might have extra bandages, while another has surplus medications.
- **Group Training:** Organize first aid workshops or CPR certification courses in your community to ensure everyone has basic skills.
- **Communication Plans:** Develop a neighborhood emergency communication system to coordinate responses and share information during crises.

Real-Life Example: During a wildfire in California, a small community pooled their medical resources and skills to treat minor injuries and manage respiratory issues caused by smoke. Their collective efforts reduced the burden on local hospitals and ensured everyone received timely care.

Adapting to Long-Term Medical Challenges

While most emergencies are short-lived, some crises can stretch on for weeks or months. Preparing for long-term medical challenges requires foresight and adaptability:

- **Chronic Conditions:** Ensure a 30- to 90-day supply of prescription medications for conditions like diabetes, asthma, or hypertension. Discuss storage options with your pharmacist to ensure medications remain effective.
- **Alternative Treatments:** Learn about natural remedies or over-the-counter alternatives for common ailments. While not a replacement for professional care, these can be helpful during prolonged disruptions.
- **Sanitation and Hygiene:** Stock up on disinfectants, hand sanitizers, and portable toilets to maintain hygiene and prevent infections during extended emergencies.

Pro Tip: Create a "medical go-bag" with essential supplies for extended evacuations. Include items like water purification tablets, high-calorie snacks, and extra first aid supplies.

By approaching medical preparedness as a holistic, ongoing process, you can ensure your family is ready for both minor injuries and major emergencies. With the right tools, skills, and mindset, you'll be able to navigate crises with confidence and control.

How to make sure you can cope with medical emergencies

Step 1: Build a Professional-Grade First Aid Kit

A well-stocked first aid kit is your first line of defense in any medical situation. Tailor it to your family's specific needs and ensure it covers a range of potential emergencies. Here's how to create a kit that's both comprehensive and practical:

- **Basic Supplies:** These items address everyday injuries like cuts, scrapes, and minor burns.
    - Adhesive bandages in various sizes
    - Sterile gauze pads and medical tape
    - Antiseptic wipes and antibiotic ointments
    - Disposable gloves to prevent infection
- **Advanced Supplies:** Essential for more serious injuries, these items can stabilize a victim until professional help arrives.
    - Tourniquets to stop severe bleeding
    - Hemostatic agents (e.g., Celox or QuikClot) to clot wounds quickly
    - Splints for fractures and dislocations
    - CPR masks for safe resuscitation
- **Medications:** Stock a variety of over-the-counter and prescription medications.
    - Pain relievers like ibuprofen and acetaminophen
    - Antihistamines for allergic reactions
    - Anti-inflammatory drugs
    - Prescription medications tailored to your family's needs

- **Specialized Items:** Depending on your household, you may need these extras:
    - Infant supplies (diapers, baby formula, baby thermometer)
    - Pet medications and first aid tools for animals

Category	Examples	Recommended Quantity
Basic Supplies	Bandages, antiseptic wipes	Multiple per type
Advanced Supplies	Tourniquet, hemostatic gauze	1-2 each
Medications	Ibuprofen, antihistamines	2-week supply

Pro Tip: Store your first aid kit in an easily accessible location, such as a hall closet or kitchen drawer, and include a manual for reference during emergencies. Have duplicates in your car and workplace for additional coverage.

Step 2: Address Common Medical Emergencies

Preparing for likely scenarios ensures you can act quickly and confidently. Here's how to address the most common medical situations:

- **Cuts and Lacerations:**
    - Clean wounds with antiseptic wipes to reduce the risk of infection.
    - Apply pressure to stop bleeding and, if necessary, use a hemostatic agent.
    - Cover the wound with a sterile bandage or dressing.
- **Sprains and Fractures:**
    - Immobilize the affected area with a splint or elastic bandage.
    - Apply ice packs to reduce swelling and pain.
    - Avoid unnecessary movement until medical help is available.
- **Burns:**
    - Cool burns with clean, cold water for at least 10 minutes to reduce pain and swelling.
    - Apply a sterile, non-adhesive dressing and avoid using creams or oils unless advised by a professional.
- **Dehydration:**
    - Keep oral rehydration salts on hand to treat dehydration caused by illness, heat, or exertion.
    - Encourage small, frequent sips of water rather than large gulps.

Pro Tip: Use color-coded or clearly labeled containers for different types of emergencies. For example, a red pouch for bleeding and a blue pouch for medications.

Step 3: Store and Protect Medical Supplies

Proper storage ensures your supplies are effective when you need them. Follow these guidelines:

- **Temperature Control:** Keep your kit in a cool, dry place to prevent medications, adhesives, and tools from degrading.
- **Airtight Containers:** Use waterproof and dustproof containers to protect supplies from moisture and contaminants. For mobile kits, consider hard cases with foam inserts.
- **Strategic Placement:** Place kits in multiple locations—at home, in your car, and at your workplace—so you're covered wherever you are.

Pro Tip: Conduct quarterly inspections to replace expired medications and ensure all supplies are in working condition.

Step 4: Acquire Essential Medical Skills

Having supplies is only half the battle—you must also know how to use them effectively. Here's how to build your skills:

- **First Aid Training:** Enroll in a certified course to learn CPR, wound care, and how to handle common injuries. Many courses also cover how to use automated external defibrillators (AEDs).
- **Scenario-Based Practice:** Simulate medical emergencies with your family to build confidence and familiarity with the kit. Practice treating cuts, applying splints, and using a tourniquet.
- **Learn Triage:** In a crisis, prioritize treatment based on severity. For example:
    - Life-threatening injuries (e.g., severe bleeding) require immediate attention.
    - Minor injuries (e.g., small cuts) can wait.

Real-Life Example: A friend of mine, a fellow SEAL, used basic first aid skills to stabilize a neighbor after a car accident. His quick actions—stopping the bleeding and keeping the injured person calm until help arrived—were the difference between life and death. That experience reinforced the value of preparedness, even in everyday life.

Step 5: Plan for Long-Term Medical Needs

In extended emergencies, you may face challenges that go beyond basic first aid.

- **Chronic Conditions:** Ensure a surplus of medications for conditions like diabetes, asthma, or high blood pressure.
- **Sanitation:** Maintain hygiene with disinfectants, hand sanitizers, and clean water to prevent infections.
- **Infections:** Include antibiotics or consult a healthcare professional about storing antibiotics for emergency use.

Step 6: Teach and Involve Your Family

Preparedness is a team effort. Involve your family in every step to ensure they're ready to act when needed:

- **Knowledge Sharing:** Teach everyone in your household how to use basic first aid items, such as bandages, antiseptic wipes, and splints.
- **Child-Friendly Supplies:** Create a smaller, child-friendly kit and teach kids age-appropriate skills, like cleaning minor cuts or using an ice pack.
- **Practice Together:** Run family drills for scenarios like choking, burns, or injuries from falls. Reinforce these practices regularly to build muscle memory.

Real-Life SEAL Insight: Training Saves Lives

In the SEALs, medical training wasn't optional—it was life-saving. Every team member knew how to handle injuries, from minor cuts to life-threatening trauma. In your home, the same principle applies: knowledge and preparation empower you to act decisively.

Medical preparedness isn't about anticipating every possible scenario—it's about being ready for the most likely ones and having the confidence to act when seconds matter. By building a comprehensive first aid kit, learning essential skills, and involving your family in the process, you can turn a potential crisis into a manageable situation. In the next chapter, we'll focus on actionable defense tactics, equipping you with strategies to protect your family and home during confrontations.

Chapter 9: Actionable Defense Tactics

Staying Ready in High-Stakes Moments

During a home invasion or crisis, having a plan is invaluable—but knowing how to act in the moment is what truly makes the difference. This chapter focuses on real-world defense tactics that are practical, effective, and adaptable to your home's layout. You don't need military training to protect your family, but you do need clarity, decisiveness, and preparation.

The Importance of Situational Readiness

Reacting effectively in emergencies often depends on preparation and awareness. Intruders rely on surprise, speed, and confusion to achieve their goals. Your job is to counteract these factors by being observant, prepared, and deliberate in your actions. Recognizing potential threats before they escalate can prevent harm and buy critical time to act.

- **Be Proactive:** Early detection of suspicious behavior can neutralize threats before they escalate. For instance, noticing unusual vehicles or subtle signs of tampering around your home allows you to respond early.
- **Stay Calm:** Maintaining composure under pressure ensures you're making rational decisions, not emotional reactions.

Real-Life Insight: A SEAL once described surviving an ambush by focusing on his training to suppress panic. At home, the same discipline applies—stay focused on your plan to navigate high-stakes situations effectively.

Building Confidence Through Preparation

Confidence in a crisis isn't about being fearless—it's about being ready. The more familiar you are with your home's layout, your tools, and your family's emergency plan, the more effectively you'll respond when seconds count.

- **Practice Makes Perfect:** Regular drills, whether for evacuations or safe room protocols, build muscle memory and reduce hesitation.
- **Adaptability:** A solid plan is essential, but flexibility to adapt to evolving circumstances is equally important.

Pro Tip: Walk through potential scenarios with your family, identifying escape routes, safe zones, and areas where defensive action might be necessary.

Leveraging Your Environment

Your home is your greatest advantage in a crisis. Use its layout and contents to your benefit:

- **Choke Points:** Narrow hallways or doorways can funnel intruders, giving you control over their movements.
- **Natural Cover:** Use furniture like sofas, tables, or kitchen counters as barriers to protect yourself.
- **Strategic Lighting:** Install motion-activated lights in key areas to disorient intruders and reveal their positions.

Real-Life Example: A homeowner strategically placed heavy furniture near an entryway, creating a natural choke point. During a break-in, this delayed the intruder long enough for the family to secure themselves in their safe room and call for help.

Psychological Deterrence

Often, the mere perception of difficulty can dissuade intruders from targeting your home. Visible signs of security, like cameras, alarms, or reinforced doors, can shift their focus elsewhere.

- **Signs of Strength:** Display security system signage prominently, even if you don't have a full system installed.
- **Behavioral Tactics:** Simple actions like turning on lights or making noise can make an intruder second-guess their actions.

Pro Tip: Dogs, even small ones, can act as effective deterrents by barking at unusual activity. Larger, trained dogs add another layer of security.

Understanding the Psychology of Intruders

Most intruders are opportunistic and aim to avoid confrontation. By understanding their mindset, you can anticipate their actions and counteract them effectively:

- **Speed and Stealth:** Intruders want to get in and out quickly. Any delay—like reinforced doors or loud alarms—increases the chance they'll abandon the attempt.
- **Targets of Opportunity:** Homes with visible vulnerabilities, like unlocked doors or poorly lit entryways, are more attractive to criminals.
- **Unpredictability:** Actions like turning on lights, shouting, or activating alarms disrupt their plans and force them to reassess.

Real-Life Insight: In SEAL operations, disrupting the enemy's expectations often gave us the upper hand. At home, surprising an intruder with loud noise or sudden light can have a similar effect.

Key Principles to Remember

- **Early Detection:** Stay vigilant and aware of your surroundings.
- **Calm Execution:** Focus on your plan and execute it methodically.
- **Use Every Advantage:** Your home's layout, tools, and even psychological tactics are assets you can leverage.

Preparation and awareness transform your home into a secure sanctuary, capable of deterring and neutralizing threats. In the next chapter, we'll explore how resilience and recovery strategies can help you bounce back and rebuild after a crisis.

How to make sure you are prepared for danger

Step 1: Recognize the Signs of Trouble

An intruder's goal is usually to act quickly and quietly, avoiding confrontation. Recognizing early warning signs can help you act before they gain the upper hand.

- **Unusual Sounds:** Pay attention to creaking doors, footsteps, or glass breaking.
- **Disruptions:** Flickering lights or tripped alarms might indicate someone is tampering with your systems.
- **Unfamiliar Vehicles:** Cars idling outside your home for extended periods could signal someone scouting your property.

Pro Tip: Install inexpensive door and window alarms that emit a loud sound when breached. These can alert you immediately to unusual activity.

Step 2: Defensive Positioning in Your Home

Your home's layout can work for or against you in a crisis. Use it to your advantage by positioning yourself strategically.

- **Know Your Exits:** Identify multiple escape routes from each room. If one is blocked, you'll have alternatives.
- **Control Choke Points:** Narrow hallways and doorways can funnel intruders, giving you control of movement.
- **Avoid Open Spaces:** Large, open areas leave you exposed. Instead, stay in corners or behind furniture for cover.

Real-Life Example:

During a mock home defense drill, a family discovered that their living room had no clear exit apart from the front door. They restructured their furniture to create a pathway to the kitchen, which led to a back door, adding a critical escape route.

Step 3: De-escalation Strategies

Not every confrontation needs to end in violence. De-escalation can often diffuse the situation and keep everyone safe.

- **Stay Calm:** Speak in a steady, firm voice to avoid escalating the intruder's emotions.
- **Create Distance:** If possible, maintain a safe distance and use furniture or walls as barriers.
- **Compliance When Necessary:** If the intruder demands material possessions and you have no immediate means of defense, comply to protect lives. Items can be replaced; lives cannot.

Pro Tip: Practice de-escalation phrases with your family, such as "Please take what you need, but don't hurt anyone," to prepare for high-stress situations.

Step 4: Defensive Tools and Their Use

Having defensive tools within reach can provide a significant advantage in a confrontation. Choose tools that align with your abilities and the needs of your household.

- **Non-Lethal Tools:**
    - **Pepper Spray:** Effective at incapacitating intruders from a safe distance. Ensure every family member knows how to use it properly.
    - **Stun Guns:** These deliver a powerful electric shock to incapacitate an attacker. Keep them charged and within easy reach.
- **Improvised Weapons:** Everyday objects can become defensive tools in a crisis.
    - Heavy flashlights, kitchen utensils, or even a chair can serve as effective deterrents when used with confidence.
- **Firearms:** If legally owned and properly trained, a firearm can provide a last line of defense.
    - Always store firearms securely and ensure every family member understands their safe use and handling.

Tool	Advantages	Limitations
Pepper Spray	Easy to use, non-lethal	Limited range
Stun Gun	Effective incapacitation	Requires close proximity
Firearm	High stopping power	Requires training

Step 5: Family Coordination and Roles

In a high-stakes scenario, chaos can be minimized when everyone knows their role.

- **Assign Roles:** Designate tasks, such as calling 911, securing younger children, or locking doors.
- **Safe Room Protocols:** Establish a procedure for gathering in the safe room, locking the door, and waiting for help.

- **Code Words:** Use a family-specific code word to signal danger or the need to retreat without alarming an intruder.

Real-Life Example:

A family I worked with created a simple plan: the eldest child would take the younger siblings to the safe room while the parents secured the home. During a practice drill, the plan worked seamlessly, reducing everyone's anxiety about what to do in a real emergency.

Step 6: When Confrontation Is Unavoidable

If you must confront an intruder, act decisively and use every advantage at your disposal.

- **Surprise:** Intruders often expect passive victims. A loud yell or unexpected action can disrupt their plans.
- **Leverage the Environment:** Use objects like chairs or doors to create barriers or disrupt the intruder's movement.
- **Commit to Action:** Hesitation can be dangerous. Once you decide to act, do so with full commitment.

Real-Life SEAL Insight: Clarity Under Pressure

In high-stakes missions, clarity is often the difference between life and death. Every SEAL is trained to remain calm and focused, even when the situation spirals. At home, this mindset is critical. Whether you're de-escalating or taking defensive action, a clear head can save lives.

Actionable defense tactics are about preparation and presence of mind. By learning to recognize threats, positioning yourself strategically, and coordinating with your family, you can handle emergencies with confidence. In the next chapter, we'll explore resilience and recovery, focusing on how to bounce back and rebuild after a crisis.

Chapter 10: Resilience and Recovery

Bouncing Back After a Crisis

Emergencies can leave more than physical damage in their wake—they can also take a toll on your emotional well-being and disrupt your family's sense of security. Recovery is about more than fixing broken windows or replacing lost items; it's about rebuilding trust, stability, and confidence. This chapter will help you navigate the aftermath of a crisis, ensuring your home and family emerge stronger than before.

The Multifaceted Nature of Recovery

Recovering from a crisis isn't just about repairing what's broken. It involves addressing the physical, emotional, and logistical impacts that emergencies leave behind. A thorough approach ensures not only a return to normalcy but also the ability to grow stronger and more resilient for future challenges.

- **Physical Impact:** Beyond structural damage, consider how your home's defenses may have been compromised. Weak points like damaged locks or breached windows must be addressed immediately.
- **Emotional Impact:** Crises can affect every member of the household differently. Children may exhibit fear or anxiety, while adults may struggle with feelings of failure or vulnerability. Open communication is key to addressing these emotions.
- **Financial and Logistical Recovery:** From insurance claims to budgeting for repairs, managing the financial aftermath is a critical aspect of resilience.

Real-Life Example: After a tornado damaged a family's home, they not only rebuilt but also upgraded their property with reinforced doors and storm shutters. This proactive approach gave them peace of mind during future storms.

The Psychological Aftermath of Emergencies

The emotional toll of a crisis can linger long after the event itself. Understanding and addressing these effects is essential for a full recovery:

- **For Children:** Young family members may internalize fear or develop anxiety about their safety. Create opportunities for them to express their feelings and involve them in recovery efforts to restore their sense of control.
- **For Adults:** Feelings of guilt, frustration, or helplessness are common after a crisis. Acknowledge these emotions and seek support from friends, family, or professionals when needed.

- **For the Household as a Whole:** Emphasize teamwork and celebrate small victories to foster a sense of unity and accomplishment.

Pro Tip: Use storytelling as a tool to process emotions. Sharing what happened, how you responded, and how you overcame challenges can be therapeutic for everyone involved.

Turning Lessons Into Strength

Every crisis is an opportunity to learn and grow. Use the experience to identify weaknesses in your home's defenses and your family's preparedness:

- **Identify Weak Points:** Was your emergency plan effective? Were there tools or supplies you lacked? Make a list of improvements to implement.
- **Reinforce Routines:** Re-establishing daily routines provides a sense of normalcy and stability, which is particularly important for children.
- **Celebrate Resilience:** Recognize the strengths your family displayed during the crisis, whether it was quick thinking, teamwork, or emotional support.

Real-Life SEAL Insight: In the SEALs, every mission was debriefed to identify what went well and what could be improved. Applying this practice at home ensures you're better prepared for future challenges.

Strengthening Bonds Through Recovery

Crises have a way of bringing families closer together. Use the recovery process as an opportunity to strengthen relationships and build trust:

- **Involve Everyone:** Assign age-appropriate tasks to each family member. Whether it's helping with cleanup or brainstorming ways to improve safety, participation fosters a sense of ownership and teamwork.
- **Create New Traditions:** Incorporate resilience-building activities into your routine. For example, make monthly emergency drills a family event.
- **Express Gratitude:** Acknowledge the efforts of each family member during the crisis. Gratitude strengthens bonds and promotes a positive mindset.

Pro Tip: Host a "recovery dinner" to celebrate milestones, such as completing repairs or implementing a new safety measure. This not only marks progress but also reinforces the value of teamwork.

Engaging Your Community in Recovery

Your family isn't alone in the recovery process. Building connections with neighbors and local organizations can enhance resilience for everyone:

- **Share Resources:** Collaborate with neighbors to pool tools, supplies, or expertise. For example, one household may have carpentry skills while another has access to backup power sources.
- **Coordinate Efforts:** Establish a neighborhood recovery plan that includes shared communication channels and emergency contacts.
- **Build Support Networks:** Emotional recovery is often easier when you have a network of people who understand what you've been through. Community events or support groups can foster this connection.

Real-Life Example: After a flood affected a small community, residents organized weekly meetings to share updates, coordinate repairs, and provide emotional support. This collective effort accelerated recovery and strengthened community bonds.

How to Rebuild Resilience After a Crisis
Step 1: Assess the Damage

Before moving forward, you need to evaluate what's been affected—both physically and emotionally.

- **Physical Damage:** Inspect your home for structural issues, broken entry points, or damaged utilities. Prioritize repairs that restore safety, like reinforcing doors or fixing broken windows.
- **Emotional Impact:** Crises can leave lasting psychological effects, particularly on children. Look for signs of anxiety, fear, or withdrawal and address them promptly.

Area of Assessment	What to Check	Action Needed
Structural Integrity	Cracks, broken windows, damaged locks	Prioritize safety repairs
Utilities	Gas lines, electrical systems	Contact professionals
Emotional Well-Being	Anxiety, nightmares, behavioral changes	Provide reassurance and counseling

Real-Life Example:

After a break-in, a family noticed their youngest child was afraid to sleep alone. By talking openly about the event and involving the child in safety improvements, like adding new locks and alarms, they helped rebuild a sense of control and security.

Step 2: Strengthen Your Home's Defenses

Every crisis is an opportunity to learn and improve. Use the experience to identify weaknesses and enhance your home's defenses.

- **Reinforce Entry Points:** Upgrade locks, add shatterproof film to windows, or install a door brace for extra security.
- **Enhance Monitoring Systems:** Install or upgrade surveillance cameras, motion detectors, and alarm systems.
- **Layer Your Defenses:** Review Chapters 3 and 4 to ensure every layer of your home's defense is optimized.

Step 3: Rebuild Trust and Routine

Crises disrupt the rhythm of daily life, and restoring normalcy is crucial for recovery.

- **Create a Routine:** Establish consistent schedules for meals, school, and bedtime to provide stability.
- **Involve Your Family:** Engage everyone in recovery efforts, whether it's cleaning up, reinforcing security, or practicing drills.
- **Address Missteps:** If your initial plan didn't work perfectly, discuss what went wrong and how to improve it together.

Pro Tip: Celebrate small victories, like completing repairs or successfully practicing a new safety drill. These milestones can help rebuild confidence.

Step 4: Manage Financial and Logistical Recovery

Recovering from a crisis often involves dealing with insurance, expenses, and repairs.

- **Document Everything:** Take photos of damage and keep receipts for repairs or replacements.
- **File Insurance Claims Promptly:** Contact your provider as soon as possible to begin the claims process.
- **Budget for Future Improvements:** Allocate resources for upgrades that increase your home's resilience, like a generator or reinforced doors.

Step 5: Foster Psychological Resilience

Crises can leave lasting scars, but they can also foster growth. Psychological resilience is about turning adversity into strength.

- **Acknowledge Emotions:** Allow yourself and your family to feel fear, anger, or sadness—it's a natural part of recovery.
- **Seek Support:** Don't hesitate to reach out to friends, neighbors, or professional counselors. Sharing experiences can help lighten the burden.
- **Focus on Growth:** Reflect on what the crisis taught you and how it strengthened your family's bond and preparedness.

Real-Life SEAL Insight: Resilience Under Pressure

In the SEALs, we faced setbacks on almost every mission—equipment failures, injuries, or unexpected challenges. The key wasn't avoiding adversity but learning from it and coming back stronger. At home, resilience means embracing setbacks as opportunities to grow.

Step 6: Stay Prepared for the Future

Once you've recovered, ensure you're better prepared for the next potential crisis.

- **Update Your Plan:** Incorporate lessons learned into your home defense strategy.
- **Maintain Readiness:** Regularly check your supplies, practice drills, and review your family's roles in emergencies.
- **Engage Your Community:** Build relationships with neighbors and local organizations to strengthen collective resilience.

Recovery isn't just about returning to normal—it's about creating a new normal that's stronger, smarter, and more secure. By assessing the damage, rebuilding trust, and learning from the experience, you turn setbacks into stepping stones.

Chapter 11: Advanced SEAL Tactics for Home Defense

Taking Home Defense to the Next Level

For those who want to take their home defense to the next level, advanced tactics inspired by Navy SEAL training can provide an additional edge. These strategies are not about paranoia or turning your home into a fortress—they're about optimizing your environment, refining your skills, and preparing for even the most unlikely scenarios. In this chapter, we'll explore techniques that SEALs use in high-stakes situations and how you can adapt them for your home and family.

The SEAL Approach to Mastery

Advanced home defense isn't about overcomplicating your plans; it's about refining the basics to perfection. SEALs achieve their high level of readiness through discipline, redundancy, and constant adaptation—principles that can be applied to home security.

- **Discipline in Routine:** Regularly inspecting your defenses, practicing drills, and staying informed ensures that your plan remains effective and evolves with changing circumstances.
- **Redundancy in Layers:** SEALs never rely on a single solution. Each layer of defense backs up the one before it, ensuring no single failure compromises the mission.
- **Adaptability in Action:** Real-life crises rarely unfold as planned. Flexibility and quick thinking are crucial to overcoming challenges.

Real-Life Insight: During one mission, my team's primary extraction route was compromised. We had three backup plans, and switching to an alternate route ensured our success. At home, similar redundancy can safeguard your family.

Transforming Your Home into a Tactical Asset

Your home is more than a shelter; it can be a strategically advantageous space when used effectively. Consider how its layout, contents, and technology can be optimized:

- **Optimize Layout:** Walk through your home with a defensive mindset. Identify choke points, blind spots, and areas that could serve as cover.

- **Use Technology Wisely:** Smart devices like motion sensors, cameras, and alarms provide both real-time information and deterrence.
- **Repurpose Everyday Items:** Heavy flashlights, sturdy chairs, and even pots or pans can serve as improvised defensive tools.

Pro Tip: Develop a detailed map of your home's interior and exterior. Mark escape routes, safe zones, and key defensive positions to familiarize yourself and your family with the most effective strategies.

Mental Toughness: The Ultimate Defense

Advanced tactics rely as much on mindset as on tools. The ability to remain calm, focused, and decisive under pressure is a hallmark of SEAL training and a critical skill in home defense.

- **Manage Stress:** Practice breathing techniques or mindfulness exercises to maintain composure in high-stress scenarios.
- **Develop Confidence:** Regularly review your plan and practice drills to build confidence in your abilities and those of your family.
- **Stay Positive:** A resilient mindset can turn setbacks into opportunities for growth. Reflect on challenges as lessons rather than failures.

Real-Life SEAL Insight: In combat, clarity under fire often determined success. At home, a calm, prepared mindset can make the difference between chaos and control.

How to Implement Advanced SEAL Tactics for Home Defense

Step 1: Develop Situational Awareness on a New Level

Advanced situational awareness goes beyond noticing your surroundings—it's about predicting patterns and anticipating threats.

- **Behavioral Observation:** Pay attention to how people behave in your neighborhood. Unusual behaviors, like someone loitering or repeatedly circling the block, can signal potential threats.
- **Environmental Cues:** Take note of small changes, such as a gate left open or unfamiliar footprints near your home.
- **Family Drills:** Create scenarios that challenge your family's observation skills. For example, during a walk, ask them to identify five changes since their last visit to that area.

Real-Life Example:

On a deployment, my team once identified an ambush site by noticing an abandoned vehicle parked at an odd angle. Small details like these can reveal larger threats.

Step 2: Secure Your Home with Redundant Layers

Redundancy ensures no single point of failure compromises your home's defenses.

- **Dual Locks on Doors:** Use two different types of locks (e.g., a deadbolt and a keyless lock) to make forced entry harder.
- **Backup Power for Alarms:** Install a battery backup for your alarm system to keep it operational during outages.
- **Reinforce Secondary Entry Points:** Basements, attic windows, and garage doors are often overlooked but vulnerable entry points.

Redundant Layer	Purpose	Application
Dual locks	Slows down forced entry	Front and back doors
Backup alarm power	Maintains functionality in outages	Alarm systems
Secondary point security	Prevents overlooked vulnerabilities	Basements, attics, garages

Step 3: Master Tactical Movement in Your Home

Moving through your home during a crisis requires strategy to avoid exposing yourself or your family.

- **Room Clearing Basics:** Learn how to safely enter and check rooms by staying close to walls and avoiding open spaces.
- **Light Discipline:** Use flashlights sparingly in low-light situations to avoid revealing your position.
- **Choke Point Control:** If intruders are in your home, guide them into narrow areas like hallways, where you can better manage their movement.

Pro Tip: Practice moving through your home at night to familiarize yourself with obstacles and blind spots.

Step 4: Establish Offense as a Last Resort

In extreme situations where confrontation is unavoidable, having a plan for defensive offense can protect your family.

- **Safe Room Defense:** Position yourself in a fortified room and call for help, only engaging if the intruder breaches the room.
- **Improvised Weapons:** Use everyday objects, like heavy tools or even kitchen utensils, if no dedicated tools are available.
- **Firearm Safety:** If you legally own a firearm, ensure you are trained and understand the laws governing its use in home defense.

Step 5: Engage in Advanced Drills and Training

Building muscle memory through repetitive training ensures you're ready when seconds count.

- **Family Scenarios:** Simulate break-ins or natural disasters to test your family's readiness.
- **Stress Training:** Practice decision-making under simulated stress, such as using timers or unexpected changes in drills.
- **Precision Tools:** Train with defensive tools like pepper spray or tasers to improve accuracy and confidence.

Real-Life Example:

A homeowner I worked with practiced "night drills," simulating a power outage combined with an intrusion. These drills improved their ability to navigate their home and coordinate actions in the dark.

Step 6: Consider Intelligence Gathering

Proactively gathering information about your neighborhood and potential threats can give you an edge.

- **Community Awareness:** Stay updated on local crime trends by attending neighborhood meetings or using community apps.
- **Surveillance Logs:** Keep a simple log of unusual activity around your property.
- **Relationships with Neighbors:** Build a network of trusted neighbors who can share information and look out for one another.

Real-Life SEAL Insight: Planning for the Worst-Case Scenario

In SEAL missions, we prepared for the worst while hoping for the best. This mindset ensured we were never caught off guard. At home, advanced tactics are about being ready for the unexpected—not living in fear, but in confidence.

By applying these advanced tactics, you elevate your home defense strategy to a professional level. With enhanced situational awareness, layered security, and tactical training, you're not just protecting your home—you're mastering the art of resilience and readiness. This concludes our journey into home defense, leaving you with the tools and mindset to secure your family and fortress against any crisis.

Chapter 12: DIY Projects for Food Independence

Crafting a Resilient Home

Achieving home independence isn't just about stockpiling supplies—it's about developing systems that allow you to adapt and thrive during emergencies or extended periods of isolation. With the right DIY projects, you can transform your home into a self-sufficient haven capable of withstanding environmental challenges, grid failures, and other crises.

This chapter dives into practical and manageable projects that you can undertake to enhance your home's sustainability, security, and resilience. From building rainwater collection systems to creating solar-powered backup grids, these projects will empower you to take control of your household's future.

Redefining Home Independence

The concept of home independence extends beyond crisis preparation. It's about embracing a lifestyle where your home becomes a source of sustenance, energy, and security. By implementing the strategies outlined in this chapter, you'll gain the ability to:

- **Reduce Dependency:** Minimize reliance on external utilities by producing your own energy, water, and food.
- **Enhance Sustainability:** Create systems that are eco-friendly and resource-efficient.
- **Build Long-Term Resilience:** Equip your home to handle prolonged emergencies or disruptions.

Whether you live in an urban apartment, a suburban neighborhood, or a rural area, these projects can be tailored to fit your space and needs.

The DIY Mindset: Turning Challenges into Opportunities

Adopting a do-it-yourself approach fosters creativity and resourcefulness. It's not just about saving money; it's about gaining skills and taking control of your home's capabilities. Here's how to get started:

- **Set Clear Goals:** Decide what you want to achieve with your projects, whether it's energy independence, food security, or water sustainability.

- **Start Small:** Tackle one project at a time to avoid becoming overwhelmed.
- **Learn Continuously:** Watch tutorials, read guides, and seek advice from others who've undertaken similar projects.

Pro Tip: Document your progress. Keeping a journal or taking photos of each step not only helps you troubleshoot but also serves as a valuable resource for future projects.

Empowering Your Family Through DIY Projects

Involve your family in these projects to foster teamwork and build practical skills. Children can learn the basics of gardening, while teens and adults can handle more complex tasks like assembling solar panels or building rainwater systems. This collaborative approach strengthens bonds and ensures everyone understands the systems in place.

Real-Life Example: A family in California transformed their backyard into a self-sustaining oasis. They built a vertical garden, installed a solar panel system, and constructed a rainwater collection setup. By working together, they not only enhanced their home's resilience but also created a shared sense of accomplishment.

How to Build a Resilient Home with DIY Projects

Step 1: Water Independence with DIY Collection and Filtration Systems

Rainwater harvesting is one of the simplest ways to secure a sustainable water source for your household. Follow these steps to set up an efficient rainwater collection system:

1. **Select a Collection Point:**
   - Use your roof as the primary collection surface. Ensure that the roof is made of non-toxic materials (avoid asbestos or lead-based coatings).
2. **Install Gutters and Downspouts:**
   - Attach high-capacity gutters to your roof and connect them to downspouts leading to a collection barrel or tank.
3. **Add a First-Flush Diverter:**
   - This device removes debris and contaminants from the initial flow of rainwater, ensuring cleaner water in your storage system.
4. **Choose Storage Solutions:**
   - Opt for food-grade barrels or large tanks. Ensure they are sealed to prevent contamination by insects or debris.
5. **Filtration and Treatment:**
   - Install a DIY filtration system using gravel, sand, and activated carbon to purify water for non-drinking purposes.
   - For potable water, use portable filters or UV sterilizers.

System Component	Estimated Cost	Key Benefit
Gutter Extensions	$50–$150	Collects rain efficiently.
Storage Barrels (50 gal)	$40–$80 each	Compact water storage.
Sand/Carbon Filters	$30–$60	Removes impurities.
UV Sterilizers	$80–$150	Ensures potable water.

Real-Life Example: A family in Texas installed a basic rainwater system and was able to store over 500 gallons during a single rainy season. This system supported their garden irrigation needs for months, reducing their dependency on municipal water.

Step 2: Generate Your Own Power

Harnessing solar energy is one of the most effective ways to ensure energy independence. Here's how to create a basic solar power system at home:

1. **Assess Energy Needs:**
    - List essential devices (lights, refrigerator, communication devices) and calculate their combined wattage.
2. **Purchase Solar Panels:**
    - Choose monocrystalline panels for efficiency or polycrystalline for affordability.
3. **Install a Charge Controller:**
    - Prevent battery overcharging and extend its life.
4. **Set Up Deep-Cycle Batteries:**
    - These store the energy collected during daylight for use at night or during power outages.
5. **Add an Inverter:**
    - Converts DC power from batteries to AC power for household appliances.

Estimated Costs for a Basic Solar Setup:

Component	Estimated Cost	Lifespan
Solar Panels (100W)	$80–$150 per panel	25 years
Charge Controller	$20–$60	5–10 years
Deep-Cycle Batteries	$100–$300	3–5 years
Inverter	$80–$200	8–12 years

Pro Tip: Position solar panels at an angle matching your latitude for optimal sunlight absorption.

Step 3: Grow Your Own Food with Vertical Gardening

Limited space doesn't mean limited gardening opportunities. Vertical gardening allows you to maximize productivity in small areas.

1. **Build a Frame:**
    - Use wooden pallets, PVC pipes, or a metal grid to create vertical tiers for plant growth.
2. **Choose the Right Plants:**
    - Opt for high-yield crops like herbs, leafy greens, strawberries, and cherry tomatoes.
3. **Install an Irrigation System:**
    - Set up a drip irrigation system for consistent watering.
4. **Use Companion Planting:**
    - Pair plants that benefit each other (e.g., basil with tomatoes) to optimize growth and deter pests.

Plant	Time to Harvest	Yield per Square Foot
Lettuce	4–6 weeks	3–5 heads
Strawberries	6–8 weeks	1–2 pounds
Basil	4–6 weeks	10–20 leaves weekly

Real-Life Example: An urban family turned their 6-foot balcony into a thriving garden, producing enough vegetables and herbs to reduce grocery trips by 30%.

Step 4: Build a DIY Backup Heating System
Rocket Stoves

Rocket stoves are highly efficient and simple to build. They burn small amounts of wood while producing substantial heat—perfect for emergency cooking or heating.

1. **Materials Needed:**
    - Fire bricks, metal tubing, and a steel drum.
2. **Assembly:**
    - Create a combustion chamber using the fire bricks.
    - Position the metal tubing to act as a chimney, directing smoke away.
3. **Usage:**
    - Use small sticks and twigs for fuel. The stove can boil water or cook food efficiently while conserving resources.

By completing these DIY projects, you'll not only make your home more self-reliant but also gain valuable skills and confidence. Each project contributes to a broader vision of sustainability, ensuring you're prepared to thrive regardless of external circumstances. Let's turn to the next chapter to explore how to integrate these systems into your daily life seamlessly.

Projects to secure food
Step 1: Build Raised Garden Beds

Raised garden beds are a versatile and efficient way to grow your own fruits and vegetables. They improve soil quality, reduce weeds, and make gardening more accessible.

Materials Needed:

- Untreated wood planks (cedar or redwood recommended for durability)
- Galvanized screws or nails
- Landscape fabric
- Quality soil mix (compost, peat moss, and vermiculite)

Step-by-Step Instructions:

1. **Choose a Location:**
    - Select a sunny area that receives at least 6 hours of direct sunlight daily.
2. **Build the Frame:**
    - Cut wood planks to your desired dimensions (e.g., 4 feet by 8 feet).
    - Assemble the frame using galvanized screws for longevity.
3. **Prepare the Ground:**
    - Remove grass or weeds from the area and lay down landscape fabric to prevent weeds from growing into the bed.
4. **Fill the Bed:**
    - Add a mix of compost, peat moss, and vermiculite for nutrient-rich soil.
5. **Plant Your Crops:**
    - Start with easy-to-grow vegetables like tomatoes, peppers, lettuce, and carrots.

Vegetable	Time to Harvest	Yield per Plant
Tomatoes	60–80 days	8–12 pounds
Lettuce	30–45 days	4–6 heads
Carrots	60–75 days	1–2 pounds

Pro Tip: Rotate crops each season to maintain soil health and reduce pest infestations.

Step 2: Start a Small-Scale Livestock Project

For those with a bit more space, small-scale livestock can provide a reliable source of protein and other essentials.

Chickens for Eggs

- **Materials Needed:**
  - Chicken coop (DIY or pre-built)
  - Chicken feed and water dispensers
  - Nesting boxes and roosting bars
- **Steps to Get Started:**

  1. **Build or Buy a Coop:**
     - Ensure the coop is predator-proof and has adequate ventilation.
     - Provide at least 3 square feet of space per chicken.
  2. **Choose Your Breed:**
     - Opt for egg-laying breeds like Rhode Island Reds or Leghorns.
  3. **Care and Maintenance:**
     - Feed chickens a balanced diet and provide clean water daily.
     - Collect eggs daily to prevent waste.

Breed	Eggs per Year	Special Features
Rhode Island Red	250–300	Hardy and low-maintenance
Leghorn	280–330	High egg production
Australorp	250–300	Friendly and good for beginners

Rabbits for Meat

- **Materials Needed:**
  - Rabbit hutch with separate nesting areas
  - Hay, pellets, and fresh vegetables for feed
- **Steps to Get Started:**

  1. **Build a Hutch:**
     - Ensure each rabbit has at least 6 square feet of space.
     - Include wire flooring for easy cleaning.
  2. **Choose Your Breed:**
     - Consider meat breeds like New Zealand Whites or Californians.
  3. **Care and Maintenance:**
     - Clean the hutch regularly and monitor for signs of illness.

Breed	Weight at Maturity	Time to Maturity
New Zealand White	9–12 pounds	8–10 weeks
Californian	8–11 pounds	8–10 weeks

Pro Tip: Rabbits are highly efficient converters of feed to meat, making them an excellent choice for small-scale protein production.

Step 3: Preserve Your Harvest

Growing and raising food is only part of the equation—preserving it ensures you can enjoy the fruits of your labor year-round.

Canning:

1. **Materials Needed:**
   o Mason jars with lids
   o Pressure canner or water bath canner
2. **Steps:**
   o Wash jars and prepare lids.
   o Fill jars with prepared food (e.g., pickles, sauces, or jams).
   o Process jars in a canner to seal them properly.

Dehydrating:

1. **Materials Needed:**
   o Food dehydrator
2. **Steps:**
   o Slice fruits, vegetables, or meats into thin pieces.
   o Place them on dehydrator trays and dry until moisture is removed.

Food Type	Preservation Method	Shelf Life
Tomatoes	Canned	1–2 years
Apples	Dehydrated	6–12 months
Rabbit Meat	Frozen/Dehydrated	6 months (frozen)

Pro Tip: Label preserved items with dates to ensure you use the oldest items first.

Step 4: Incorporate Aquaponics

Aquaponics combines fish farming and hydroponics, creating a closed-loop system that grows vegetables and raises fish simultaneously.

How It Works:

1. Fish waste provides nutrients for plants.
2. Plants filter the water, which returns clean to the fish tank.

Materials Needed:

- Fish tank (50 gallons or more)
- Water pump and grow bed
- Tilapia or catfish (hardy fish for beginners)
- Plants like lettuce, basil, or spinach

Steps to Build:

1. **Set Up the Tank:**
   o Position the fish tank below the grow bed.
   o Install a water pump to cycle water between the two.
2. **Add Plants:**
   o Place plants in net pots filled with clay pebbles or similar medium.
3. **Introduce Fish:**
   o Add hardy fish that can thrive in varied water conditions.

Component	Cost Range	Function
Fish Tank (50 gal)	$50–100	Houses the fish
Water Pump	$30–50	Circulates water
Grow Bed	$40–80	Supports plant growth

Real-Life Example: A teacher in Arizona built a small aquaponics system in his backyard, producing 50 pounds of tilapia and a steady supply of greens annually.

DIY food projects are more than just practical—they're empowering. By growing and preserving your own food, you gain independence, reduce waste, and create a healthier lifestyle for your family. The next chapter will explore energy-efficient methods for maintaining your home's resilience, ensuring your systems are sustainable for the long term.

Chapter 13: Energy Efficiency for Sustainable Living

Maximizing Efficiency for Resilient Homes

Achieving energy efficiency is about more than just reducing your electricity bills—it's a pathway to long-term sustainability and independence. In today's world, where resources are strained and environmental concerns grow, making your home energy-efficient is a responsible and empowering choice. Small changes in how you use, conserve, and generate energy can make an outsized impact on both your financial health and your resilience during crises.

This chapter dives into strategies and DIY solutions that optimize your home's energy usage, transforming waste into opportunity and ensuring every watt counts. From improving insulation to harnessing renewable energy sources, these methods empower you to take charge of your home's energy future.

The Importance of Energy Efficiency in a Crisis

During power outages or emergencies, inefficient energy systems can turn minor inconveniences into major disruptions. Imagine trying to heat your home with leaky windows or relying on inefficient appliances when every watt of backup power is precious. By enhancing efficiency, you stretch your resources further and make your home less dependent on external systems, such as the power grid.

Energy-efficient homes are not only better equipped to handle crises but also help reduce your environmental footprint. Lowering energy consumption reduces greenhouse gas emissions, contributing to a cleaner, more sustainable future for everyone.

Key Benefits of an Energy-Efficient Home

1. **Cost Savings**:
2. Energy efficiency lowers utility bills, making more funds available for other essentials. For instance, switching to LED lighting can reduce lighting costs by up to 80%.
3. **Environmental Impact**:
4. By using less energy, you reduce demand on fossil fuels, leading to fewer carbon emissions. Over time, this contributes to a healthier planet.
5. **Increased Comfort**:

6. Proper insulation, efficient heating, and cooling systems ensure consistent indoor temperatures, eliminating drafts and hot spots.
7. **Enhanced Resilience**:
8. Energy-efficient homes are better prepared for emergencies, conserving resources like backup power during outages or natural disasters.

Common Energy Wastes in Homes

Many homes unknowingly waste significant energy due to inefficiencies. Identifying these areas is the first step to improvement:

- **Leaky Windows and Doors**: Drafts can account for up to 25% of your home's heat loss.
- **Outdated Appliances**: Older appliances often use more energy than modern ENERGY STAR-certified models.
- **Uninsulated Attics or Walls**: Poor insulation allows heat to escape in winter and enter in summer, driving up energy use.
- **Phantom Energy**: Electronics left plugged in consume power even when turned off, contributing to unnecessary costs.

Setting Energy Efficiency Goals

Before diving into upgrades, set clear, measurable goals for your home. Consider the following questions:

- **What are your primary energy needs?**
- Focus on areas like heating, cooling, and lighting, which account for the majority of energy consumption.
- **What's your budget for improvements?**
- Start with low-cost solutions like weatherstripping, then invest in larger upgrades, such as solar panels or insulation, as funds allow.
- **What are your long-term plans?**
- If you plan to stay in your home for years, prioritize durable, high-return investments like spray foam insulation or a smart thermostat.

Breaking Down Energy Efficiency by Zones

To maximize results, approach energy efficiency by focusing on specific areas of your home:

1. **The Envelope**: This includes walls, windows, doors, and the roof—everything that separates your indoor space from the outdoors. Sealing and insulating these areas prevents heat transfer, keeping your home comfortable year-round.
2. **Energy Systems**: Heating, ventilation, air conditioning (HVAC), and water heaters are some of the largest energy consumers. Modernizing these systems can drastically cut energy use.
3. **Electronics and Appliances**: From refrigerators to televisions, upgrading to efficient models reduces electricity use and minimizes phantom energy draw.

4. **Lighting**: Lighting accounts for about 15% of a typical home's electricity use. Switching to LEDs and using smart systems can make a noticeable difference.

Building a Holistic Approach

Energy efficiency is most effective when viewed as a whole-home strategy. By combining efforts across multiple areas, such as insulation, renewable energy, and efficient appliances, you amplify the impact. This layered approach also builds redundancy—if one system fails, others can pick up the slack, ensuring your home remains functional and comfortable.

How to: Transform Your Home into an Energy-Efficient Powerhouse

Step 1: Improve Home Insulation

Proper insulation minimizes heat loss in winter and retains cool air in summer, significantly reducing energy consumption.

Key Areas to Insulate:

1. **Walls and Ceilings:**
    - Install fiberglass or foam insulation in walls and attic spaces to prevent temperature fluctuations.
2. **Windows and Doors:**
    - Use weatherstripping or caulking to seal gaps.
    - Add thermal curtains to windows for added insulation.
3. **Floors:**
    - Lay rugs or carpets in draft-prone areas. For more permanent solutions, install underfloor insulation.

Insulation Type	Cost per Square Foot	Energy Savings (%)
Fiberglass Batts	$0.30–$0.50	20–30
Spray Foam	$1.00–$3.00	30–50
Weatherstripping	$0.10–$0.50	10–20

Pro Tip: Conduct a home energy audit using an infrared thermometer to identify heat loss areas.

Step 2: Install Energy-Efficient Lighting

Lighting accounts for a significant portion of energy use. Upgrading to efficient systems can dramatically reduce this burden.

Steps to Upgrade Lighting:

1. **Switch to LED Bulbs:**
    - LEDs consume up to 80% less energy than incandescent bulbs and last up to 25 times longer.
2. **Use Motion Sensors:**
    - Install motion-activated lights in high-traffic areas to avoid unnecessary use.
3. **Install Smart Lighting Systems:**
    - Use app-controlled lights to schedule operation and remotely turn off unused fixtures.

Bulb Type	Average Lifespan (Hours)	Energy Usage (Watts)	Annual Savings (per Bulb)
Incandescent	1,000	60	–
Compact Fluorescent	10,000	15	$5
LED	25,000	8	$7

Real-Life Example: A homeowner replaced all 30 incandescent bulbs in their home with LEDs, saving approximately $200 annually on energy bills.

Step 3: Optimize Heating and Cooling Systems

Heating and cooling systems are the largest energy consumers in most homes. Simple upgrades can lead to significant savings.

DIY Projects:

1. **Install a Programmable Thermostat:**
    - Schedule heating and cooling to match occupancy patterns.
2. **Seal HVAC Ducts:**
    - Use duct tape or mastic sealant to eliminate air leaks in ductwork.
3. **Ceiling Fans:**
    - Reverse fan direction in winter to push warm air down and circulate it effectively.

Upgrade	Cost	Estimated Savings (%)
Programmable Thermostat	$50–$200	10–15
Duct Sealing	$100–$300	20–25
Ceiling Fan Installation	$50–$150	5–10

Pro Tip: Keep HVAC filters clean to maintain efficiency and air quality.

Step 4: Integrate Renewable Energy Sources

Renewable energy systems like solar panels and wind turbines reduce dependency on the grid while shrinking your carbon footprint.

Small-Scale Solar Projects:

1. **Solar Water Heaters:**
    - Install rooftop panels to heat water using sunlight.
2. **Portable Solar Chargers:**
    - Charge small devices like phones and tablets with portable solar panels.

Wind Turbines:

- Suitable for rural areas with consistent wind speeds.
- Combine with solar panels for a hybrid system.

Renewable Source	Startup Cost	Annual Savings
Solar Panels (1 kW)	$2,000–$5,000	$200–$500
Wind Turbine (1 kW)	$3,000–$8,000	$300–$600
Solar Water Heater	$1,000–$3,000	$150–$350

Real-Life Example: A household in Arizona installed a 3 kW solar panel system, which reduced their annual electricity bill by 75%, recouping the investment in just seven years.

Step 5: Harvest Passive Energy

Passive energy systems use natural resources to maintain comfort without mechanical systems.

1. **Passive Solar Heating:**
    - Position south-facing windows to maximize sunlight in winter.
    - Install thermal mass materials like concrete or stone to store and radiate heat.
2. **Rainwater Harvesting:**
    - Integrate rain barrels into your gutter system to collect and reuse water for irrigation.
3. **Natural Ventilation:**
    - Open windows on opposite sides of the home to create cross-ventilation.

Pro Tip: Plant deciduous trees near windows to provide shade in summer and allow sunlight in winter.

Step 6: Reduce Phantom Energy

Phantom energy, also known as standby power, refers to electricity consumed by devices that are turned off but still plugged in.

Steps to Eliminate Phantom Energy:

1. **Use Smart Power Strips:**
    - Automatically cut power to devices when not in use.

2. **Unplug Chargers:**
    - Disconnect phone and laptop chargers when not actively charging.
3. **Upgrade Appliances:**
    - Replace old electronics with ENERGY STAR-certified models.

Device	Standby Power (Watts)	Annual Cost
TV	10	$12–20
Game Console	8	$10–15
Desktop Computer	15	$20–25

Real-Life Example: A small office implemented smart power strips for their equipment, cutting standby energy use by 40% and saving $150 annually.

Energy efficiency isn't just about cutting costs—it's about creating a sustainable and resilient home. By improving insulation, optimizing energy systems, and integrating renewables, you can reduce your environmental footprint while gaining independence. The next chapter will delve into advanced water management systems, further enhancing your home's self-reliance and sustainability.

Chapter 14: Mastering Water Management for Total Independence

The Lifeblood of Self-Sufficiency

Water is the cornerstone of survival and the foundation of any self-sufficient lifestyle. It's not just about having enough water to drink; it's about creating a reliable system that ensures access to clean, usable water for all aspects of daily life—from cooking and cleaning to irrigation and livestock care. In times of crisis, water becomes the most valuable resource. Mastering water management is about more than survival; it's about creating a sustainable, efficient system that integrates seamlessly into your self-sufficient lifestyle.

Expanding Beyond the Basics

1. Understanding Water Availability

Water availability is not guaranteed, even in areas with high annual rainfall. Seasonal variations, regional droughts, and infrastructure failures can all disrupt supply. A comprehensive understanding of your local water sources—including rain, rivers, groundwater, and municipal systems—ensures you can design a robust plan tailored to your environment.

2. Integrating Water Management into Everyday Life

Water management isn't just a crisis skill; it's a daily practice. Incorporating efficient habits like mindful usage, strategic reuse, and waste reduction not only conserves resources but also strengthens your long-term independence.

3. Anticipating Challenges

Even the most prepared systems can encounter obstacles. Algae growth in storage tanks, contamination in catchment systems, or unexpected overuse can all jeopardize water quality and quantity. Anticipating these challenges and designing systems with built-in redundancies ensures your household remains resilient.

Innovative Water Management Concepts

1. Advanced Rainwater Harvesting Techniques

Standard rainwater collection systems can be enhanced for greater efficiency and versatility.

- **Multiple Catchment Areas:** Utilize not only rooftops but also other surfaces like sheds or carports to increase collection capacity.
- **Underground Storage:** Install subterranean tanks to save space and maintain cooler temperatures, which inhibit bacterial growth.

2. Greywater Integration into a Closed-Loop System

Move beyond basic greywater recycling to create a fully integrated system. Combine greywater with composting systems for garden irrigation, or use advanced filtration to repurpose it for toilet flushing or laundry.

3. Emergency Water Sources and Strategies

In prolonged crises where primary systems fail, unconventional sources such as condensation collection, groundwater pumps, or emergency desalination become critical. Develop a clear plan for locating and utilizing backup sources.

How to Master Water Management for Total Independence

Step 1: Evaluate Your Water Needs

The amount of water you require depends on your household size, lifestyle, and environment.

- **Drinking Water:** Allocate at least one gallon per person per day for drinking and basic hygiene.
- **Cooking and Cleaning:** Plan for an additional 0.5 to 1 gallon per person per day for food preparation and dishwashing.
- **Special Needs:** Account for pets, medical conditions, and gardening.

Category	Daily Requirement (Per Person)	Notes
Drinking and Hygiene	1 gallon	Minimum for survival and comfort.
Cooking and Cleaning	0.5–1 gallon	Depends on meal prep requirements.
Pets (Small/Medium)	0.25–0.5 gallon	Varies by species and size.

Step 2: Build a Resilient Water Collection System

Rainwater Harvesting

Harnessing rainwater is one of the most effective ways to secure an independent water supply.

- **Set Up Collection Points:** Use rooftops with non-toxic materials as catchment surfaces.
- **Install First-Flush Diverters:** Divert debris and contaminants from initial runoff before water enters storage.
- **Storage Tanks:** Use food-grade, UV-resistant barrels or tanks to prevent contamination and algae growth.

Greywater Recycling

Reuse lightly used water from sinks, showers, and washing machines for non-potable applications like irrigation.

- **Filtration:** Install a basic sand or charcoal filter to remove debris.
- **Application:** Divert greywater to gardens, lawns, or composting systems.

Step 3: Purify Water for Safe Consumption

Raw water, even from seemingly clean sources, can carry harmful pathogens. Use these purification methods:

- **Boiling:** The most reliable method. Boil water for at least 1 minute (or 3 minutes at higher altitudes).
- **Filtration Systems:** Use portable filters or countertop units to remove bacteria, protozoa, and sediments.
- **Chemical Treatment:** Chlorine tablets or iodine drops are effective for killing microbes in emergency situations.
- **DIY Charcoal Filter:** Layer sand, activated charcoal, and gravel in a container to create a low-cost, effective filter.

Method	Cost	Effectiveness	Best Use
Boiling	Free	99.99% pathogen elimination	Small batches, emergencies
Portable Filters	$30–$100	Removes bacteria and protozoa	Camping or travel
Chemical Treatment	$10–$50	Effective but alters taste	Short-term emergencies
DIY Charcoal Filter	$20–$40	Removes impurities, basic pathogens	Non-potable applications

---

Step 4: Store Water Safely

Long-term water storage requires careful planning to maintain quality.

- **Containers:** Use BPA-free, food-grade plastic containers or stainless steel tanks.
- **Location:** Store in a cool, dark place to prevent bacterial growth and plastic degradation.

- **Preservation:** Add water treatment solutions, such as unscented bleach (8 drops per gallon), to inhibit microbial growth.

Storage Example for a Family of Four (2-Week Supply)

Container Size	Number Required	Total Capacity
5-gallon jugs	12	60 gallons
55-gallon drum	1	55 gallons

Step 5: Optimize Usage During Emergencies

Water conservation is critical during a crisis.

- **Reuse Water:** Repurpose greywater for tasks like flushing toilets or watering plants.
- **Monitor Consumption:** Track daily usage to ensure your supply lasts the expected duration.
- **Prioritize Needs:** Allocate water to essential activities like drinking and sanitation first.

Real-Life Example: A Drought-Resilient Household

A family in California, facing frequent droughts, implemented a rainwater harvesting system combined with greywater recycling. With 1,000 gallons of storage capacity and efficient filtration, they reduced their reliance on municipal water by 50%.

Mastering water management is a critical step toward home sustainability. By evaluating your needs, implementing reliable collection and purification systems, and optimizing usage, you can ensure a steady supply of clean water even in challenging circumstances. In the next chapter, we'll explore strategies for creating a fully integrated, self-sufficient home ecosystem.

Chapter 15: Creating a Fully Self-Sufficient Home Ecosystem

Designing for Independence

Creating a self-sufficient home is about more than just preparing for emergencies—it's about cultivating a sustainable lifestyle that allows you to thrive independently from external systems. Designing an ecosystem within your home ensures that energy, water, food, and waste systems work together seamlessly. This chapter focuses on how to assess your home's unique potential, implement integrated systems, and create a sustainable environment that supports your family's long-term resilience.

Expanding Your Vision of Independence

1. Holistic Resource Management

True self-sufficiency means understanding the interplay between energy, water, and food systems. Each resource supports the others in a cycle of efficiency: energy powers your tools, water nourishes your plants, and waste transforms into valuable compost for your food supply. Designing your home around this synergy is the key to sustainability.

2. Anticipating Environmental Challenges

Every location presents unique opportunities and challenges. Whether you face cold winters, dry climates, or frequent storms, your home's design should adapt to local conditions. For example, homes in drought-prone areas should prioritize water conservation systems, while those in colder climates need robust insulation and passive heating solutions.

3. Futureproofing Through Scalable Systems

Design systems that can evolve with your needs. Starting small, such as with a single solar panel or raised garden bed, allows you to expand over time without overwhelming your budget or resources. This approach ensures long-term sustainability while minimizing initial costs.

How to Design a Self-Sufficient Home Ecosystem

Step 1: Assess Your Home's Capabilities

Before implementing self-sufficient systems, conduct a thorough assessment of your property's potential:

Key Factors to Consider:

- **Available Space:** Determine how much land or indoor space you can dedicate to food production, water systems, and energy generation.
- **Sunlight Exposure:** Evaluate roof angles, yard orientation, and window placement for solar energy and gardening potential.
- **Local Climate:** Understand seasonal changes and weather patterns to optimize heating, cooling, and food production.
- **Existing Infrastructure:** Identify upgrades needed for insulation, water storage, and energy systems.

Pro Tip: Use free tools like solar calculators and planting zone maps to analyze your property's strengths and limitations.

Step 2: Build Integrated Energy Systems

Energy independence is foundational to a self-sufficient home. Combining renewable energy sources with efficient storage ensures you have power year-round.

1. Solar Power:

- Install photovoltaic panels to generate electricity. Pair them with a battery bank to store excess energy.
- Use solar water heaters for hot water needs, reducing reliance on electricity or gas.

2. Wind Power:

- For properties with consistent wind speeds, install small-scale wind turbines. Combine with solar systems for hybrid energy production.

3. Backup Solutions:

- Keep a propane generator or portable power station as a secondary energy source during peak demand or maintenance periods.

Energy Source	Benefits	Challenges
Solar Panels	Renewable, low maintenance	High initial cost
Wind Turbines	Efficient in windy areas	Requires steady wind
Battery Banks	Reliable energy storage	Limited lifespan, costly

Real-Life Example: A rural household in Montana combined a 5 kW solar array with a 2 kW wind turbine, powering their entire home and storing surplus energy for emergencies.

Step 3: Develop Sustainable Water Systems

A fully self-sufficient home needs integrated water systems to collect, store, and purify water efficiently.

1. Rainwater Harvesting:

- Install gutters and downspouts connected to storage tanks. Use first-flush diverters to filter debris.

2. Greywater Recycling:

- Redirect water from sinks, showers, and laundry to irrigate gardens or flush toilets. Add basic filters for safe reuse.

3. Backup Water Sources:

- Drill a well if local regulations permit, and use a manual or solar-powered pump.

System	Key Components	Estimated Cost
Rainwater Harvesting	Tanks, gutters, filters	$500–$2,000
Greywater Recycling	Diverters, filters, piping	$300–$1,000
Well System	Pump, storage, filtration	$5,000–$15,000

Pro Tip: Use gravity-fed systems for irrigation to reduce reliance on pumps and electricity.

Step 4: Establish Self-Sustaining Food Production

1. Food Forests:

- Transform part of your yard into a food forest with layers of edible plants, from fruit trees to herbs.
- Combine perennials like asparagus and rhubarb with annual crops for year-round harvests.

2. Hydroponics and Aquaponics:

- Use hydroponic systems to grow leafy greens and herbs indoors with minimal water.
- Pair aquaponics with fish farming, where fish waste nourishes plants, and plants filter the water for fish.

3. Small-Scale Livestock:

- Raise chickens for eggs, rabbits for meat, or bees for honey.
- Incorporate portable coops and rotational grazing to maintain land health.

System	Advantages	Challenges
Food Forest	Low maintenance, diverse yield	Requires time to establish
Hydroponics	Efficient, space-saving	Requires monitoring
Small-Scale Livestock	Protein source, waste recycling	Predators, upkeep

Real-Life Example: An urban family in Seattle built a compact aquaponics system in their garage, producing 40 pounds of tilapia and fresh vegetables annually.

Step 5: Implement Efficient Waste Management

1. Composting:

- Convert kitchen scraps and yard waste into nutrient-rich compost for gardens.
- Use a dual-bin system to separate fresh waste from finished compost.

2. Humanure Toilets:

- Composting toilets turn human waste into safe, usable fertilizer when processed correctly. Use sawdust or wood shavings to control odors.

3. Recycling:

- Set up sorting stations for paper, glass, metal, and plastic. Ensure proper disposal of hazardous materials like batteries.

Waste System	Benefit	Setup Cost
Composting	Enriches soil, reduces waste	$50–$300
Composting Toilets	Saves water, produces fertilizer	$500–$2,000
Recycling Station	Reduces landfill impact	$100–$500

Pro Tip: Worm composting (vermiculture) is an excellent way to break down food scraps quickly in small spaces.

Step 6: Integrate Smart Home Technology

Smart technology can streamline self-sufficient systems and provide real-time data for better resource management.

Examples of Smart Integrations:

- **Energy:** Monitor solar panel output and battery levels using apps.
- **Water:** Automate irrigation systems based on weather forecasts.
- **Security:** Use smart cameras and sensors to protect your property and resources.

Pro Tip: Choose devices with offline capabilities to maintain functionality during internet outages.

Creating a self-sufficient home ecosystem requires effort, but the rewards are unparalleled. By integrating renewable energy, sustainable water systems, food production, and efficient waste management, you build a home that not only meets your needs but also contributes to a healthier planet. In the next chapter, we'll explore advanced strategies for long-term resilience and adapting to future challenges.

Chapter 16: Advanced Strategies for Long-Term Resilience

Thriving in the Face of Uncertainty

Long-term resilience isn't just about weathering a crisis—it's about emerging stronger and better prepared for what lies ahead. The ability to adapt, optimize, and expand your self-sufficient systems transforms survival into sustainable living. This chapter focuses on advanced strategies for creating a lifestyle that not only endures but flourishes in the face of uncertainty.

Beyond Basics: The Resilience Mindset

1. Anticipating Future Challenges

Preparing for the long term requires more than simply addressing today's needs. As technology evolves, environmental conditions shift, and unforeseen events arise, maintaining adaptability ensures your systems remain effective. For instance:

- **Climate Change Impacts:** Rising temperatures and unpredictable weather patterns may affect water availability or crop yields.
- **Geopolitical Instability:** Supply chain disruptions could limit access to tools, seeds, or energy components.
- **Aging Infrastructure:** Regular upgrades and replacements keep systems running smoothly over decades.

2. Building Skills Over Stockpiles

Stockpiling supplies is a short-term solution. True resilience lies in developing skills that allow you to grow, repair, and innovate as circumstances change. Learn to:

- Repair solar panels and battery banks.
- Identify and preserve local heirloom seeds.
- Design modular systems that adapt to new needs.

3. Leveraging the Power of Community

While self-sufficiency begins at home, a resilient community amplifies individual efforts. Collaborating with neighbors or joining local resilience networks ensures shared resources, knowledge, and protection during crises.

How to Implement Advanced Strategies for Long-Term Resilience

Step 1: Develop a Long-Term Resource Plan

Planning for sustainability over months or even years requires a clear understanding of your resource needs and how to replenish them.

1. Calculate Sustainable Consumption Rates:

- **Water:** Identify average daily use for your household and establish systems to replenish supplies through rainwater harvesting and filtration.
- **Energy:** Monitor energy usage patterns and expand renewable energy systems to meet peak demands.
- **Food:** Focus on high-yield, nutrient-dense crops and establish rotational planting schedules.

Resource	Daily Need (Per Person)	Replenishment Method
Water	1.5–2 gallons	Rainwater, filtration, greywater reuse
Energy	5–8 kWh	Solar, wind, backup generators
Food (Calories)	2,000	Gardens, livestock, preserved stores

2. Stockpile Strategically:

- Rotate supplies to ensure freshness and usability.
- Invest in durable storage solutions that protect against pests and environmental damage.

Pro Tip: Create a digital inventory to track quantities, expiration dates, and usage patterns for all critical resources.

Step 2: Master Advanced Food Production Techniques

Scaling your food systems ensures long-term resilience, even in extended crises.

1. Perennial Food Systems:

- Plant fruit and nut trees, berry bushes, and perennial vegetables to provide reliable annual yields with minimal maintenance.
- Examples: Apple trees, blueberries, asparagus, and rhubarb.

2. Advanced Hydroponics and Aquaponics:

- Build scalable systems to grow high-value crops like lettuce, spinach, and herbs indoors or in small spaces.

- Pair aquaponics with fish species like tilapia or catfish for dual-purpose protein and nutrient-rich plant growth.

3. Seed Saving and Crop Rotation:

- Save seeds from heirloom varieties to reduce dependency on external suppliers.
- Rotate crops to maintain soil fertility and prevent pest buildup.

Technique	Benefit	Challenge
Perennial Food Systems	Consistent yield, low maintenance	Longer establishment time
Hydroponics/Aquaponics	Space-efficient, year-round	Requires monitoring
Seed Saving	Cost-effective, sustainable	Requires knowledge of genetics

Real-Life Example: A small homestead in Oregon used a combination of perennial fruit trees and aquaponics to produce 70% of their family's food supply within five years.

Step 3: Strengthen Community Connections

No one survives alone. Building relationships with neighbors and local networks enhances both security and resource availability.

1. Establish Bartering Networks:

- Trade excess goods like eggs, vegetables, or firewood for items you lack.
- Use community forums, social media groups, or local meetups to connect with like-minded individuals.

2. Share Knowledge and Resources:

- Host workshops on gardening, canning, or renewable energy systems.
- Join or create co-ops for bulk purchasing of seeds, tools, and supplies.

3. Build Security Alliances:

- Coordinate with neighbors to monitor properties and share emergency plans.
- Develop communication protocols for emergencies using two-way radios or community alert systems.

Pro Tip: Regularly practice community drills to strengthen bonds and improve collective readiness.

Step 4: Prepare for Worst-Case Scenarios

Sometimes, unforeseen events require extra measures. Advanced preparation ensures you're ready for even the most extreme situations.

1. Build a Bug-Out Plan:

- Identify safe locations within a 100-mile radius and map multiple routes to reach them.
- Pack comprehensive go-bags with essentials for at least 72 hours.

2. Create Redundant Systems:

- Have backups for critical systems like water purification, energy generation, and food storage.
- Maintain both high-tech and low-tech solutions to cover all contingencies.

3. Train for Self-Defense:

- Take advanced courses in self-defense and firearm safety.
- Practice situational awareness and de-escalation techniques.

Scenario	Preparation Strategy	Example Tool/System
Natural Disaster	Evacuation plan, backup power	Portable generator
Grid Failure	Off-grid energy, water systems	Solar panels, manual pumps
Security Breach	Safe room, alarm systems	Motion sensors, cameras

Real-Life Example: A family in Florida maintained a bug-out location in the mountains and successfully evacuated ahead of a hurricane, avoiding harm and property loss.

Step 5: Regularly Test and Adapt Your Systems

Preparedness is a dynamic process. Regular testing and adaptation keep your systems effective.

1. Conduct Mock Drills:

- Simulate scenarios like power outages, water shortages, or home invasions to identify weaknesses.
- Involve every family member in practice sessions to reinforce roles and procedures.

2. Stay Informed:

- Monitor local and global trends for emerging threats, such as climate change impacts or geopolitical instability.
- Adjust your systems accordingly.

3. Document Lessons Learned:

- Keep a preparedness journal to track what works, what doesn't, and how to improve.

Pro Tip: Update your plans and systems at least annually, incorporating new technologies or techniques as they become available.

Long-term resilience isn't a single goal—it's a mindset. By integrating these advanced strategies into your daily life, you create a home and lifestyle capable of weathering any storm. The journey to self-sufficiency is ongoing, but every step forward brings greater security, independence, and peace of mind.

Chapter 17: Scaling Your Self-Sufficient Lifestyle

Beyond Your Four Walls

Becoming self-sufficient is a journey, not a destination. Once you've mastered creating a sustainable home, the natural next step is to expand those efforts outward. Scaling your lifestyle means thinking beyond your immediate household, envisioning a community of shared resources, sustainable practices, and mutual support. By increasing your capacity, inspiring others, and fostering cooperation, you can transform self-sufficiency into a movement that benefits not just your family but your neighbors and local community.

Why Scale Your Self-Sufficient Lifestyle?

Scaling your efforts offers several key benefits:

- **Increase Resilience**: Expanding systems like food production or renewable energy strengthens your ability to weather extended crises.
- **Reduce Waste**: Larger systems often allow you to utilize resources more effectively, such as preserving surplus food or sharing energy with others.
- **Foster Community**: Sharing knowledge and resources creates bonds, improving collective preparedness and fostering a sense of unity.
- **Generate Income or Barter Value**: Surplus goods and skills can become valuable commodities, creating opportunities for additional income or barter.

Scaling isn't about taking on more than you can handle—it's about leveraging what you've learned to create a broader, more impactful version of your self-sufficient lifestyle.

Key Areas for Expansion

1. Food Production: From Backyard to Homestead

Once your home garden is running efficiently, consider scaling food production to support more than just your household. Increasing capacity enables you to store food for long-term use, share with others, or even sell at local markets.

- **Beyond the Garden**: Add greenhouses for year-round growth, expand to larger crops like grains or legumes, or integrate fruit orchards.
- **Protein Sources**: Diversify livestock with chickens, goats, or rabbits for eggs, milk, and meat. Consider aquaculture for raising fish.

- **Community Farming**: Partner with neighbors to manage larger plots of land cooperatively, sharing labor and resources.

2. Energy Systems: Scaling Sustainability

Energy independence doesn't have to stop at meeting your family's needs. With scaled systems, you can generate surplus power to share or sell, fostering resilience at the community level.

- **Microgrid Collaboration**: Work with neighbors to create a shared energy system. These decentralized networks are more reliable during outages and reduce dependency on traditional utilities.
- **Passive Income**: Surplus energy from expanded solar or wind systems can be sold back to the grid in many areas, generating additional income.
- **Advanced Storage**: Larger battery banks or advanced technologies like Tesla Powerwalls allow for greater energy retention and usage flexibility.

3. Bartering and Local Economies

Creating a barter-based economy enhances resilience by reducing reliance on cash and external systems. Scaling your lifestyle means fostering a network of trade that benefits everyone.

- **Skills Exchange**: Beyond trading goods, offer services like repair work, teaching, or professional skills in return for items you need.
- **Community Markets**: Organize or participate in regular local markets where people can exchange food, crafts, and skills without the need for currency.
- **Resource Sharing**: Pool resources like tools, equipment, and expertise to maximize collective efficiency.

4. Knowledge Sharing and Education

Scaling self-sufficiency isn't just about increasing production—it's about empowering others to follow your lead. Sharing your experiences can inspire a ripple effect, amplifying the impact of your efforts.

- **Workshops and Classes**: Teach practical skills, from gardening to DIY energy systems, to help others gain confidence in their abilities.
- **Content Creation**: Use social media, blogs, or YouTube to document your journey, sharing tips, tutorials, and inspiration for a wider audience.
- **Mentorship Programs**: Guide newcomers through the process of becoming self-sufficient, offering one-on-one support and advice.

Community as a Foundation for Scaling

The Power of Collective Resilience

Scaling self-sufficiency isn't just about what you can achieve individually—it's about building networks that strengthen everyone involved. Imagine a neighborhood where one household provides surplus eggs, another produces solar power, and a third offers carpentry skills. Together, you create a system that's far more resilient than any single family could achieve alone.

- **Shared Resources**: Create community tool libraries, seed banks, or shared storage for bulk food supplies.
- **Emergency Preparedness Networks**: Collaborate with neighbors to develop evacuation plans, shared shelters, and pooled emergency supplies.
- **Community Advocacy**: Work with local leaders to prioritize sustainability initiatives, such as funding for renewable energy or the establishment of cooperative gardens.

Real-Life Inspiration

Scaling your self-sufficient lifestyle can have profound, real-world results. Consider the case of a family in Oregon that expanded their garden to include greenhouses and diversified livestock. Not only did they become completely food independent, but they also began hosting community workshops and sharing surplus produce at local markets. Their efforts inspired others in the area, creating a network of families committed to sustainable living.

By scaling your systems, sharing your knowledge, and fostering a collaborative spirit, you contribute to a more resilient and sustainable community. The next chapter will explore cutting-edge technologies and how they can further enhance your efforts toward a self-sufficient, future-proof lifestyle.

How to Expand Your Self-Sufficient Lifestyle and Build Community Resilience

Step 1: Expand Food Production Systems

Scaling food production ensures surplus for preservation, sharing, or bartering.

1. Increase Garden Output:

- Expand your growing area with additional raised beds or vertical gardens.
- Transition to high-yield crops like potatoes, squash, and beans to maximize calorie production.

2. Incorporate Greenhouses:

- Build a greenhouse to extend your growing season and protect crops from harsh weather.

- Use solar heating or passive thermal systems to maintain temperature control.

3. Diversify Livestock:

- Add larger animals, such as goats or sheep, for milk, meat, or wool.
- Explore aquaculture to raise fish like tilapia or catfish in larger quantities.

System	Benefits	Challenges
Expanded Gardens	Increased food variety	Requires additional space
Greenhouses	Year-round growing capacity	Initial investment costs
Livestock Diversification	Protein, milk, and fiber sources	Higher maintenance needs

Real-Life Example: A family in Wisconsin scaled their 1-acre garden into a 5-acre homestead, producing enough food to sell at local farmers' markets while sustaining their household.

Step 2: Enhance Renewable Energy Systems

Greater energy independence supports increased production and offers opportunities to share power with neighbors.

1. Add Capacity:

- Expand your solar panel array or wind turbine setup to produce surplus energy.
- Install larger battery banks to store additional power.

2. Explore Microgrids:

- Create a neighborhood microgrid to share energy resources with trusted neighbors.
- Use blockchain-based energy tracking systems to monitor contributions and usage.

3. Generate Passive Income:

- Sell excess power back to the grid if your utility company offers buyback programs.
- Rent out portable solar generators or battery packs to your community.

Energy Upgrade	Benefit	Setup Cost
Additional Solar Panels	Greater energy independence	$2,000–$5,000
Microgrid Development	Shared resources, cost savings	Varies by size and tech
Battery Bank Expansion	Longer energy storage capacity	$1,000–$3,000

Pro Tip: Use energy monitoring apps to identify patterns and optimize system performance.

Step 3: Establish a Bartering Economy

Sharing resources and skills creates a resilient local economy that benefits everyone.

1. Identify Bartering Opportunities:

- Trade excess produce, preserved foods, or livestock products for tools, clothing, or services.
- Offer specialized skills, such as carpentry or first aid training, in exchange for other goods.

2. Organize Bartering Events:

- Host monthly meetups where neighbors can exchange goods and services.
- Use social media or community boards to promote events and attract participants.

3. Create a Local Currency System:

- Develop a points-based or token system to facilitate trades.
- Ensure transparency and accountability to maintain trust.

Item/Skill	Barter Potential	Example Exchange
Fresh Eggs	High demand, easy to trade	1 dozen eggs for hand tools
Carpentry Skills	Valuable for repairs	Build shelves for canned goods
Herbal Remedies	Increasingly popular	Salves for seeds or produce

Real-Life Example: A small town in Oregon revived a bartering economy during a prolonged power outage, exchanging essential goods like food, firewood, and medical supplies.

Step 4: Teach and Inspire Others

Sharing your knowledge creates a ripple effect, empowering others to adopt self-sufficient practices.

1. Host Workshops:

- Teach skills like canning, composting, or building DIY energy systems.
- Partner with local schools or community centers to reach a wider audience.

2. Start a Blog or YouTube Channel:

- Share your journey, successes, and lessons learned to inspire others.
- Provide step-by-step guides, tips, and resources for beginners.

3. Mentor Newcomers:

- Offer one-on-one guidance to neighbors or friends interested in self-sufficiency.

- Create a support group where members can exchange ideas and troubleshoot challenges together.

Pro Tip: Document your workshops and projects to create a library of resources for future use.

Step 5: Advocate for Community Resilience

Larger-scale resilience initiatives can benefit entire neighborhoods or towns, ensuring collective survival and prosperity.

1. Engage Local Leaders:

- Advocate for policies that support renewable energy, community gardens, and emergency preparedness programs.
- Collaborate with city planners to integrate sustainability into local infrastructure.

2. Establish Community Projects:

- Create shared spaces, such as tool libraries, seed banks, or cooperative gardens.
- Build emergency supply depots accessible to all residents.

3. Develop Resilience Plans:

- Work with neighbors to draft a community-wide disaster preparedness plan.
- Include evacuation routes, communication protocols, and resource-sharing strategies.

Initiative	Impact	Implementation
Community Gardens	Increases food access	Use vacant lots, shared effort
Tool Libraries	Reduces costs for individuals	Centralized location, donations
Emergency Supply Depots	Enhances disaster readiness	Stockpile basics collectively

Real-Life Example: A neighborhood in Florida organized a community garden and supply depot that became a lifeline during hurricane season, providing fresh produce and emergency kits.

Scaling your self-sufficient lifestyle goes beyond personal preparedness. By expanding systems, engaging with your community, and sharing knowledge, you contribute to a more resilient and sustainable world. The next chapter will explore advanced techniques for integrating modern technology with self-sufficient practices to push your efforts even further.

Chapter 18: Integrating Modern Technology with Self-Sufficient Practices

Bridging the Gap Between Tradition and Innovation

The journey toward self-sufficiency has long relied on time-tested techniques, from growing food to harvesting rainwater. However, modern technology now offers tools that can amplify these practices, making them more efficient, scalable, and effective. Whether you're a seasoned homesteader or just starting your self-sufficiency journey, integrating technology can help you save time, reduce waste, and maximize results.

This chapter dives into how technology can transform your approach to energy, food, water, and home management, allowing you to achieve sustainability without compromising on comfort or convenience.

The Advantages of Tech-Enhanced Self-Sufficiency

Modern tools and systems bring significant benefits to sustainable living, including:

- **Automation:** Reducing manual labor while improving precision and consistency.
- **Data Insights:** Enabling informed decisions through real-time monitoring and analytics.
- **Scalability:** Making it easier to expand systems as your needs grow.
- **Resource Optimization:** Minimizing waste and maximizing efficiency.

By balancing traditional practices with cutting-edge innovations, you can ensure your lifestyle remains resilient in the face of evolving challenges.

Core Principles of Tech Integration

1. Efficiency Without Dependency

The goal of incorporating technology is to enhance—not replace—your ability to be self-reliant. While automation and advanced tools can streamline processes, always have low-tech backups in case of system failures or power outages. For example, pair automated irrigation systems with manual watering tools or keep basic filtration methods alongside advanced purification systems.

2. Modular Design for Flexibility

When integrating technology, choose systems that can evolve with your needs. A modular approach allows you to add components or upgrade features without overhauling your entire setup. For instance, start with a basic solar panel array and expand it as your energy demands increase.

3. Data as a Tool for Growth

Track the performance of your systems and use the data to make informed decisions. Analytics can reveal inefficiencies, predict maintenance needs, and help you plan for future expansions. Embrace apps and software that consolidate data into user-friendly dashboards for a comprehensive overview of your home's performance.

Technology in Practice: Key Applications

Energy Systems

Integrating modern renewable energy technology ensures consistent power supply and reduces reliance on external grids.

- **Smart Grids for Your Home:** Use AI-powered systems to allocate energy efficiently, directing power where it's most needed.
- **Hybrid Solutions:** Combine solar, wind, and backup generators for a robust, multi-layered energy system.
- **Energy Recycling:** Capture excess heat from appliances or generators and redirect it to heat water or living spaces.

Food Production

Technology can revolutionize how you grow, monitor, and harvest food.

- **Precision Agriculture:** Use sensors to measure soil moisture, nutrient levels, and crop health. These tools allow you to apply water or fertilizer only where it's needed, reducing waste.
- **Indoor Farms:** Automate climate control, lighting, and watering in indoor gardens or greenhouses to achieve year-round production.
- **Robotics:** Small-scale robotic systems can automate planting, weeding, and harvesting tasks.

Water Management

Water scarcity is an increasing concern, and technology offers solutions to optimize its use.

- **Smart Water Storage:** Monitor tank levels and automate distribution for irrigation or household use.
- **Real-Time Quality Testing:** Sensors can continuously test water quality, alerting you to contaminants and adjusting purification processes.
- **Greywater Recycling Systems:** Advanced filtration systems can treat greywater for reuse in gardens or non-potable household tasks.

Real-Life Examples of Tech-Enhanced Practices

1. **The Automated Homestead:**

   A family in Oregon installed a system that monitors their energy production, food growth, and water usage via a single dashboard. With smart irrigation and solar-powered sensors, they cut water usage by 40% and doubled crop yields within a year.

2. **Aquaponics for Sustainability:**

   In an urban setting, a couple combined an automated aquaponics system with AI-powered grow lights, producing fresh vegetables and fish while using 90% less water than traditional gardening.

Challenges and Solutions in Tech Integration

Challenge 1: Initial Costs

Advanced systems often require a significant upfront investment.

Solution: Start small with scalable systems, like modular solar panels or basic hydroponic setups, and expand over time.

Challenge 2: Technology Overload

Too many disconnected systems can create inefficiency and confusion.

Solution: Use a centralized hub or app to integrate all smart devices and systems for seamless management.

Challenge 3: Maintenance Complexity

High-tech systems may require specialized repairs or replacements.

Solution: Educate yourself on basic maintenance tasks and keep critical spare parts on hand.

Future-Proofing Your Tech Integration

Adopt Emerging Technologies

Keep an eye on advancements such as blockchain for resource tracking, AI for predictive analytics, and nanotechnology for improved filtration and energy storage.

Community-Based Solutions

Explore tech-enabled cooperative systems, like neighborhood microgrids or shared tool libraries, to pool resources and knowledge.

Sustainable Upgrades

Ensure that the materials and technologies you choose align with your long-term goals. For example, prioritize recyclable components, renewable energy compatibility, and systems that reduce waste.

How to Integrate Technology with Self-Sufficient Practices

Step 1: Leverage Smart Home Technology

Smart home devices can automate tasks, optimize resource usage, and provide critical data for better decision-making.

1. Energy Monitoring Systems:

- Use smart meters to track real-time energy consumption and identify inefficiencies.
- Pair with apps that provide actionable insights to reduce waste.

2. Automated Irrigation:

- Install smart irrigation controllers that adjust watering schedules based on weather forecasts and soil moisture levels.
- Connect to your rainwater harvesting system for a closed-loop solution.

3. Security Enhancements:

- Use smart cameras, motion detectors, and door sensors to protect your property.
- Monitor your home remotely through smartphone apps for added peace of mind.

Device	Purpose	Cost Range
Smart Thermostat	Optimizes heating/cooling	$100–$300
Soil Moisture Sensor	Prevents overwatering	$20–$50
Smart Security Camera	Enhances home security	$50–$200

Pro Tip: Integrate all smart devices into a central hub (e.g., Alexa, Google Home) for streamlined management.

Step 2: Utilize Advanced Renewable Energy Systems

Expanding and refining your energy systems ensures greater independence and resilience.

1. Solar Panel Upgrades:

- Opt for bifacial solar panels, which capture sunlight on both sides for increased efficiency.
- Use microinverters to optimize energy production from each panel.

2. Wind Energy Optimization:

- Add vertical-axis wind turbines for urban or smaller properties with variable wind patterns.
- Combine wind systems with battery banks to store excess power.

3. Energy Storage Innovations:

- Upgrade to lithium-iron-phosphate (LiFePO4) batteries for longer lifespan and safety.
- Explore vehicle-to-grid (V2G) technology, using electric vehicles as mobile energy storage.

Technology	Benefit	Estimated Cost
Bifacial Solar Panels	Higher efficiency	$200–$400 per panel
Vertical-Axis Wind Turbine	Compact, urban-friendly	$2,000–$5,000
LiFePO4 Batteries	Longer lifespan, safer storage	$1,000–$3,000 per unit

Real-Life Example: A rural family in Iowa upgraded their solar array with bifacial panels and added a vertical-axis wind turbine, increasing energy production by 40%.

Step 3: Integrate Hydroponics and Automation

Hydroponic systems, enhanced with automation, offer efficient and high-yield food production with minimal water usage.

1. Automated Hydroponic Systems:

- Use sensors to monitor pH levels, nutrient concentrations, and water temperature.
- Connect systems to smartphone apps for remote management.

2. Vertical Farming Units:

- Install vertical racks with LED grow lights to maximize indoor growing space.
- Pair with automated irrigation and nutrient delivery systems.

3. AI-Powered Growing Assistants:

- Utilize AI-driven apps that provide planting schedules, growth predictions, and pest control advice.

System	Advantages	Cost Range
Automated Hydroponics	Reduced labor, higher yields	$500–$2,000
Vertical Farming Units	Space-efficient, scalable	$1,000–$5,000
AI Growing Apps	Data-driven decision-making	$10–$50 monthly

Pro Tip: Use recycled materials to build DIY hydroponic systems for a cost-effective solution.

Step 4: Explore Cutting-Edge Water Management Tools

Advanced technologies can improve water collection, purification, and conservation.

1. Atmospheric Water Generators (AWGs):

- Extract water from the air using dehumidification technology.
- Ideal for arid regions or during water shortages.

2. Smart Filtration Systems:

- Install multi-stage filters with real-time monitoring for impurities and flow rate.
- Use UV sterilizers to eliminate bacteria and viruses.

3. Leak Detection Sensors:

- Place sensors near water systems to detect leaks early and prevent wastage.

Technology	Application	Cost Range
Atmospheric Water Generator	Water extraction from air	$2,000–$8,000
Smart Filtration System	Continuous clean water supply	$500–$1,500
Leak Detection Sensors	Prevents water damage	$20–$100 per sensor

Real-Life Example: An off-grid home in Arizona installed an AWG and reduced reliance on municipal water by 30%, even during a prolonged drought.

Step 5: Embrace Data-Driven Decision Making

Using data analytics ensures continuous improvement and efficiency in your systems.

1. Resource Tracking:

- Use apps to monitor energy, water, and food production levels.
- Analyze data trends to adjust usage and optimize resource allocation.

2. Predictive Maintenance:

- Employ IoT sensors to detect wear and tear in critical systems, such as solar panels or pumps.
- Schedule maintenance proactively to prevent system failures.

3. AI Integration:

- Implement AI algorithms to predict weather patterns, optimize planting schedules, or simulate resource needs during emergencies.

Pro Tip: Combine data from multiple systems into a centralized dashboard for a holistic view of your home's performance.

Integrating modern technology into self-sufficient practices opens new possibilities for efficiency, scalability, and innovation. By embracing these tools, you ensure your lifestyle is not only sustainable but also adaptable to the challenges of the future. In the next chapter, we'll explore strategies for building a lasting legacy of preparedness and inspiring future generations to embrace independence and resilience.

Chapter 19: Building a Legacy of Preparedness

Introduction: Passing the Torch

True self-sufficiency is about more than preparing for the present—it's about ensuring that the values, systems, and knowledge you've built continue to benefit future generations. This chapter focuses on creating a sustainable and enduring legacy of preparedness, fostering a culture that prioritizes resilience, and inspiring others to adopt these principles in their own lives.

By teaching skills, creating durable systems, and embedding self-sufficiency into your family's and community's values, you're not only protecting your legacy but also contributing to a world that values independence and sustainability.

The Importance of Legacy in Preparedness

Leaving a legacy of preparedness isn't just about the physical systems you build—it's about the mindset and knowledge you impart to others. Your efforts should aim to:

- **Empower Future Generations:** Equip them with the tools and skills they need to adapt and thrive.
- **Promote Sustainable Practices:** Ensure that your systems and values align with long-term environmental and social sustainability.
- **Foster Collective Resilience:** Strengthen your community's ability to support one another in times of need.

Core Principles for Creating a Lasting Legacy

1. Lead by Example

Demonstrating the benefits of a prepared lifestyle is the most effective way to inspire others. Show that resilience is not just practical but also rewarding and fulfilling.

2. Focus on Knowledge Transfer

Skills, strategies, and insights are far more valuable than tools alone. Equip others with the know-how to build and maintain systems themselves.

3. Build Adaptable Systems

The world changes, and so must your legacy. Create systems that can evolve with technological advances, environmental conditions, and the needs of future generations.

Key Areas for Legacy Building

1. Education Across Generations

Teaching is the cornerstone of a lasting legacy. Create opportunities to share your knowledge with both family members and the broader community.

- **Hands-On Learning:** Involve children in age-appropriate tasks like planting seeds, maintaining tools, or using simple DIY systems.
- **Workshops for Adults:** Offer practical lessons on advanced systems like aquaponics or solar maintenance.
- **Storytelling for Impact:** Use personal anecdotes to explain the importance of preparedness, making abstract concepts relatable.

2. Durable, Scalable Systems

A legacy is only as strong as the infrastructure you leave behind. Invest in high-quality, long-lasting materials and design systems that future generations can expand or modify as needed.

- **Energy Systems:** Build solar and wind energy setups with future expansion in mind.
- **Water Systems:** Design rainwater collection and filtration systems that are easy to scale.
- **Food Production:** Plant perennial crops and establish gardens that grow stronger over time.

3. Community Engagement

A prepared community is more resilient than any single household. Engage your neighbors and local organizations to create a shared culture of preparedness.

- **Shared Projects:** Build tool libraries, seed banks, or cooperative gardens.
- **Knowledge Exchanges:** Host skill-sharing events or forums where participants can learn from each other.
- **Mutual Aid Networks:** Organize systems for resource sharing during emergencies.

Real-Life Inspirations

1. **Generational Gardening:** A family in Vermont passed down their heirloom seed collection and crop rotation methods for over four generations, preserving both biodiversity and knowledge.
2. **Community Resilience Hub:** In Texas, a neighborhood converted a vacant lot into a preparedness center with shared tools, a communal garden, and an emergency supply depot.

3. **Preparedness Workshops:** A retired engineer in California hosted annual workshops on renewable energy, inspiring dozens of families to adopt solar power systems.

How to Build a Legacy of Preparedness

Step 1: Educate the Next Generation

Sharing knowledge with younger generations ensures the continuation of self-sufficient practices.

1. Teach Practical Skills:

- Involve children and teens in daily activities, such as gardening, preserving food, and maintaining systems.
- Use age-appropriate tools and methods to build confidence and competence.

2. Create Learning Opportunities:

- Organize hands-on workshops or DIY projects for kids.
- Incorporate storytelling to explain the importance of resilience and self-reliance.

3. Develop an Educational Archive:

- Document your systems, processes, and lessons in a format that future generations can access, such as journals, videos, or digital files.

Skill	Recommended Age Group	Teaching Method
Gardening Basics	5–10 years	Plant small, fast-growing crops
Food Preservation	10–16 years	Teach canning and dehydration
Solar System Maintenance	16+ years	Hands-on repairs and monitoring

Real-Life Example: A homestead in Maine created a family "Preparedness Book" with guides, recipes, and diagrams, which has been passed down for three generations.

Step 2: Build Durable Systems

Design systems that require minimal upkeep and can endure over time.

1. Focus on Longevity:

- Choose high-quality materials for projects, such as stainless steel for water tanks or UV-resistant solar panels.
- Perform regular maintenance to prevent premature wear and tear.

2. Implement Redundancies:

- Create backups for critical resources like water, energy, and food storage.

- Ensure multiple layers of security and fail-safes for essential systems.

3. Plan for Scalability:

- Design systems that can grow with your family's needs.
- Leave detailed instructions for expanding gardens, adding livestock, or upgrading energy systems.

System	Durability Features	Expected Lifespan
Solar Panels	UV-resistant, tempered glass	25–30 years
Rainwater Tanks	Stainless steel, sealed caps	20+ years
Composting Toilets	High-quality plastic, manual parts	15–20 years

Pro Tip: Keep a log of maintenance schedules and repairs for future reference.

Step 3: Create a Preparedness Culture

Fostering a culture of preparedness within your community ensures collective resilience.

1. Host Community Events:

- Organize preparedness fairs or skill-sharing workshops.
- Create forums or groups for discussing sustainability and resilience.

2. Recognize Contributions:

- Celebrate milestones, such as the installation of a new solar system or the completion of a large harvest.
- Use these opportunities to inspire others to contribute and learn.

3. Lead by Example:

- Showcase your systems and successes through tours or open-house days.
- Be transparent about challenges to build trust and encourage problem-solving together.

Real-Life Example: A small town in Colorado developed a preparedness network, where families shared resources like seeds, tools, and knowledge, creating a self-reliant community hub.

Step 4: Pass Down Your Knowledge

Preserving your expertise ensures that future generations can build upon your foundation.

1. Write a Family Preparedness Manual:

- Include detailed guides on systems like rainwater harvesting, solar energy, and food preservation.
- Use diagrams, photos, and step-by-step instructions for clarity.

2. Record Video Tutorials:

- Demonstrate complex tasks, such as repairing solar panels or building a greenhouse.
- Store videos on multiple platforms to ensure longevity.

3. Host Legacy Days:

- Dedicate time to teach family members or community groups about key systems.
- Combine hands-on training with Q&A sessions for deeper understanding.

Method	Best For	Example Content
Written Manuals	Reference over time	Maintenance schedules
Video Tutorials	Visual learners	Step-by-step system builds
Legacy Days	Interactive learning	Multi-system overviews

Pro Tip: Use cloud storage and physical backups to preserve important documents and videos.

Step 5: Inspire Future Generations

Instilling values of sustainability and resilience ensures that your legacy grows beyond your immediate family.

1. Promote Sustainability Values:

- Encourage mindfulness about resource use, recycling, and conservation.
- Highlight the benefits of a self-sufficient lifestyle, such as cost savings and environmental stewardship.

2. Support Educational Initiatives:

- Sponsor local schools or youth programs to introduce self-sufficiency concepts.
- Donate resources like books, tools, or seeds to community projects.

3. Encourage Innovation:

- Motivate future generations to improve existing systems with new technologies.
- Celebrate creative solutions to challenges in self-sufficiency.

Real-Life Example: A family in New Mexico created an annual "Preparedness Challenge" for local youth, offering prizes for innovative ideas like DIY water filters and energy-efficient designs.

Building a legacy of preparedness is about more than passing down tools and systems—it's about fostering a mindset of independence, creativity, and responsibility. By educating future generations, creating durable systems, and inspiring your community, you ensure that your efforts continue to make a difference for decades to come. In the final chapter, we'll reflect on the journey toward self-sufficiency and explore how to keep adapting as the world evolves.

Chapter 20: Advanced Survival Scenarios and Strategies

Thriving in the Unpredictable

In the face of extreme scenarios, survival transcends mere preparation—it requires adaptability, innovative thinking, and a calm, calculated approach. While foundational preparedness ensures stability, advanced strategies can transform crises into manageable challenges. This chapter focuses on how to prepare for and navigate extraordinary situations like extended grid failures, natural disasters, civil unrest, and prolonged isolation. By applying these advanced techniques, you'll cultivate resilience and confidence in the face of uncertainty.

Beyond Basic Preparedness

1. Expanding Your Toolkit

Advanced survival situations often demand tools and resources beyond the basics. High-efficiency systems like solar-powered water purifiers, multi-fuel generators, and durable emergency shelters offer an edge during prolonged emergencies.

2. Strategic Mindset

Survival in extreme conditions isn't just about what you have—it's about how you think. Prioritize decision-making frameworks that emphasize risk assessment, prioritization, and adaptability. A calm, focused mind under pressure can mean the difference between a crisis and a manageable situation.

3. Building Mental and Emotional Resilience

Mental stamina is as vital as physical resources in advanced scenarios. Fear, isolation, or fatigue can hinder decision-making. Developing techniques to maintain morale, such as mindfulness practices or engaging in structured routines, keeps you focused on solutions rather than obstacles.

Core Advanced Strategies

1. Proactive Planning

The most successful survivalists anticipate challenges before they arise. Regularly revisit and refine your plans to address evolving risks and personal circumstances.

2. Tactical Resource Management

In prolonged emergencies, resources like fuel, food, and water must be carefully rationed to last the duration of the crisis. Advanced resource tracking systems, including digital apps or meticulous physical records, can prevent shortages.

3. Training for Real-World Scenarios

Practical experience often outshines theoretical knowledge. Conducting realistic drills—such as simulated power outages, medical emergencies, or evacuation scenarios—ensures your household is equipped to respond effectively.

How to Navigate Advanced Survival Scenarios and Strategies

Step 1: Prolonged Power Outages

When the grid fails for weeks or months, maintaining energy, food, and communication becomes critical.

1. Energy Conservation:

- Prioritize essential appliances like refrigerators and medical devices.
- Use LED lanterns and battery-powered devices for lighting.

2. Alternative Power Sources:

- Rely on backup systems like solar panels or wind turbines.
- Use portable generators sparingly and safely to avoid fuel depletion.

3. Communication Solutions:

- Maintain battery-powered radios for news updates.
- Invest in satellite phones for emergency communication.

Tool	Purpose	Cost Range
LED Lanterns	Efficient lighting	$20–$50
Portable Generator	Short-term power backup	$500–$2,000
Satellite Phone	Reliable emergency communication	$600–$1,200

Pro Tip: Store extra fuel and battery packs, and rotate them regularly to ensure usability.

Step 2: Natural Disasters

Extreme weather events like hurricanes, earthquakes, or floods require immediate action and preparation.

1. Evacuation Plans:

- Map out multiple evacuation routes from your home.
- Pack go-bags with essentials such as water, food, first aid supplies, and identification.

2. Securing Your Home:

- Reinforce doors and windows to withstand strong winds or debris.
- Elevate valuables and electronics in flood-prone areas.

3. Emergency Sheltering:

- Identify safe locations within your home (e.g., basements, interior rooms).
- Stockpile items like blankets, non-perishable food, and potable water.

Scenario	Key Preparation	Recommended Supplies
Hurricane	Secure windows, evacuate if needed	Sandbags, tarps
Earthquake	Create safe zones	Emergency whistle, helmets
Flood	Elevate valuables, seal basements	Waterproof containers, pumps

Real-Life Example: A family in Florida used sandbags and plywood to protect their home from a hurricane, minimizing damage and preserving essential supplies.

Step 3: Civil Unrest

Unrest can lead to disruptions in essential services and threaten personal safety.

1. Home Fortification:

- Install reinforced locks and security cameras.
- Keep a low profile by minimizing visible wealth, such as luxury vehicles or electronics.

2. Personal Safety:

- Avoid public areas and maintain situational awareness.
- If safe, coordinate with trusted neighbors for mutual protection.

3. Resource Stockpiling:

- Ensure a three-month supply of food, water, and medical supplies.
- Avoid hoarding visibly; store items discreetly.

Security Measure	Benefit	Estimated Cost
Reinforced Locks	Deters unauthorized entry	$50–$200
Security Cameras	Monitors property	$100–$500
Safe Room Supplies	Enhances protection	Varies based on setup

Pro Tip: Establish a trusted communication network to stay informed and coordinate efforts.

Step 4: Extended Isolation

Whether due to a pandemic or remote living, prolonged isolation requires careful planning to maintain physical and mental health.

1. Food and Water Management:

- Rotate preserved food stocks to maintain freshness.
- Use water filtration systems to extend potable water supplies.

2. Mental Health Strategies:

- Establish daily routines to create a sense of normalcy.
- Stay connected with loved ones through phone or video calls.

3. Skill Development:

- Use downtime to learn new skills, such as gardening, carpentry, or first aid.
- Encourage family members to engage in group activities, such as cooking or crafting.

Challenge	Solution	Example Activity
Food Fatigue	Experiment with preserved ingredients	Canned food recipes
Loneliness	Regular virtual meetups	Weekly video calls
Idle Time	Productive hobbies	DIY projects, skill building

Real-Life Example: During a harsh winter in Alaska, a remote family used planned activities and skill-sharing to maintain morale and improve their homestead's functionality.

Step 5: Advanced Medical Preparedness

In extreme scenarios, professional medical help may not be immediately available. Advanced planning can save lives.

1. Build a Comprehensive Medical Kit:

- Include items such as sutures, tourniquets, and antibiotics.
- Learn how to use advanced supplies through training courses.

2. Telemedicine:

- Enroll in telemedicine services to consult with healthcare professionals remotely.
- Keep a list of symptoms and treatments for common conditions.

3. Long-Term Health Management:

- Stockpile prescription medications and maintain a detailed health history for each family member.
- Practice preventative care through proper nutrition, exercise, and hygiene.

Medical Supply	Purpose	Cost Range
Tourniquets	Stops severe bleeding	$20–$50
Antibiotics	Treats infections	Varies, consult provider
Telemedicine Access	Remote healthcare guidance	$50–$150 annually

Pro Tip: Regularly practice medical scenarios to ensure everyone in your household is familiar with basic emergency procedures.

Advanced survival scenarios require more than basic preparedness—they demand adaptability, foresight, and resourcefulness. By mastering these strategies, you not only safeguard your household but also ensure that you are equipped to face the most challenging situations with confidence. The journey to self-sufficiency and resilience doesn't end here—it's a lifelong commitment to learning, adapting, and thriving no matter what the future holds.

Chapter 21: The Economics of Self-Sufficiency

Introduction: Financial Independence Through Sustainability

Embracing a self-sufficient lifestyle is more than a strategy for survival—it's a pathway to financial freedom. By reducing dependency on external systems, creating surplus resources, and investing in sustainable infrastructure, you can transform your home into an economic powerhouse. This chapter delves into the financial aspects of self-sufficiency, showcasing how to save money, generate income, and build long-term financial resilience.

The Financial Case for Self-Sufficiency

1. Breaking Free from Rising Costs

In times of inflation, supply chain disruptions, or economic uncertainty, the cost of food, energy, and utilities can skyrocket. A self-sufficient lifestyle shields you from these fluctuations. Producing your own food, harvesting rainwater, and generating renewable energy not only reduces monthly bills but also protects you from volatile market conditions.

2. Turning Savings Into Investments

The savings generated from reducing reliance on external systems can be reinvested into expanding self-sufficient infrastructure. Over time, these investments pay for themselves through reduced costs and new income streams.

3. Contributing to a Circular Economy

By creating and using resources within your home, you minimize waste and contribute to a sustainable economy. Bartering and selling surplus products further strengthens local economies, fostering community resilience.

How to Master the Economics of Self-Sufficiency

Step 1: Analyze Cost Savings

1. Reduced Living Expenses:

- **Food:** Growing your own fruits, vegetables, and raising livestock drastically cuts grocery bills.
- **Energy:** Renewable energy systems reduce or eliminate electricity costs.
- **Water:** Rainwater harvesting and greywater recycling lower utility bills.

2. Avoiding External Dependencies:

- Avoid price surges during shortages by producing your own resources.
- Minimize costs for repairs and services by learning DIY skills.

Expense Category	Typical Cost (Monthly)	Self-Sufficient Alternative	Savings
Groceries	$500	Homegrown produce and meat	$200–$300
Electricity	$150	Solar and wind energy	$100–$150
Water	$50	Rainwater systems	$30–$40

Pro Tip: Track expenses before and after implementing self-sufficient systems to quantify savings.

Step 2: Generate Income From Surplus Resources

1. Sell Homegrown Products:

- **Fresh Produce:** Sell excess vegetables, fruits, and herbs at local farmers' markets or to neighbors.
- **Livestock Products:** Market eggs, milk, honey, or meat.
- **Preserved Foods:** Create value-added goods like jams, pickles, or dehydrated snacks.

2. Offer Services:

- Host workshops on gardening, food preservation, or DIY energy systems.
- Rent out equipment, such as tillers or solar generators, to neighbors.

3. Expand Into E-Commerce:

- Use platforms like Etsy or Amazon Handmade to sell handmade goods or specialty products.
- Offer online consultations or courses for those interested in self-sufficiency.

Resource	Potential Product/Service	Estimated Income
Vegetables	Fresh produce boxes	$20–$50 per week
Eggs	Dozen packs	$5–$8 per dozen
Workshops	Teaching skills	$50–$200 per session

Real-Life Example: A suburban family in Michigan earns an additional $5,000 annually by selling surplus honey and hosting beekeeping workshops.

Step 3: Invest in Durable Systems

Reinvesting savings and income into high-quality infrastructure ensures long-term financial stability.

1. Prioritize Long-Term Value:

- Purchase durable, low-maintenance equipment like stainless steel water tanks or high-efficiency solar panels.
- Opt for perennial crops and low-maintenance livestock to reduce recurring costs.

2. Build Scalable Systems:

- Design systems that can expand with demand, such as modular solar arrays or additional garden beds.
- Allocate a portion of profits toward scaling up production or upgrading technology.

3. Maintain What You Build:

- Schedule regular maintenance for critical systems to avoid costly repairs.
- Stockpile spare parts and tools to perform repairs independently.

System	Investment	Expected Lifespan
Solar Panel Array	$5,000–$15,000	25–30 years
Water Storage Tanks	$500–$2,000	20+ years
Perennial Food Forest	$1,000–$3,000	Decades (with maintenance)

Pro Tip: Use warranties and service agreements to protect your investments.

Step 4: Leverage Tax Incentives and Grants

1. Renewable Energy Credits:

- Many governments offer tax credits or rebates for solar panels, wind turbines, and energy-efficient appliances.
- Research local, state, and federal programs to maximize benefits.

2. Agricultural Grants:

- Apply for grants designed to support small-scale farming or sustainable practices.
- Programs often cover equipment, seeds, or infrastructure improvements.

3. Education and Training Support:

- Subsidies may be available for attending workshops or certifications related to sustainability and self-sufficiency.

Incentive Program	Eligibility	Benefit
Solar Investment Tax Credit	Solar panel installation	30% of total cost
USDA Microloans	Small farmers	Up to $50,000
Energy Efficiency Rebates	Home upgrades	Varies by region

Real-Life Example: A homestead in Oregon offset 40% of their solar installation costs through state and federal incentives, reducing their payback period by five years.

Step 5: Plan for Financial Resilience

1. Create an Emergency Fund:

- Set aside funds for unexpected expenses, such as system repairs or medical emergencies.
- Aim to save at least three to six months' worth of essential expenses.

2. Diversify Income Streams:

- Combine multiple revenue sources, such as product sales, workshops, and consulting.
- Invest in passive income opportunities, like renting out land or equipment.

3. Insure Critical Assets:

- Protect high-value systems, like renewable energy setups or livestock, with appropriate insurance policies.
- Ensure coverage extends to natural disasters or theft.

Strategy	Benefit	Implementation
Emergency Fund	Covers unexpected costs	Save 10% of monthly income
Diversified Income	Reduces financial risk	Combine active/passive streams
Insurance Policies	Protects investments	Consult with local providers

Pro Tip: Periodically review financial plans to adjust for changes in income, expenses, or goals.

The economics of self-sufficiency go beyond saving money—they offer a blueprint for financial independence and resilience. By reducing costs, generating income, and reinvesting in sustainable systems, you can build a lifestyle that is both secure and rewarding. The journey doesn't end here—keep exploring new opportunities to expand your efforts and inspire others to follow suit.

Chapter 22: Preparing for a Sustainable Future

Introduction: Shaping Tomorrow Today

Sustainability is more than an immediate solution—it is a commitment to a thriving, resilient future. In an era of increasing environmental and economic challenges, adopting a forward-thinking approach is essential. This chapter explores strategies to navigate global uncertainties, harness innovative technologies, and foster collective resilience while ensuring a sustainable legacy for future generations.

The Path to Sustainable Resilience

The challenges of climate change, resource scarcity, and shifting economies demand proactive solutions. Addressing these issues requires rethinking traditional systems, embracing innovation, and building networks of support that extend beyond individual households.

Why Sustainability Matters

- **Environmental Preservation:** Protecting ecosystems ensures the availability of essential resources like clean water and arable land.
- **Economic Stability:** Sustainable practices reduce long-term costs and provide insulation from market volatility.
- **Community Well-Being:** Resilient communities can better withstand crises and recover more quickly.

How to Prepare for a Sustainable Future

Step 1: Understand Future Challenges

Anticipating potential risks enables proactive planning and adaptation.

1. Climate Change Impacts:

- Increased frequency of extreme weather events, such as hurricanes, droughts, and wildfires.
- Shifts in growing seasons and crop viability.

2. Resource Scarcity:

- Declining availability of fresh water and arable land.
- Rising costs and shortages of essential goods, such as food and energy.

3. Economic and Social Instability:

- Volatile markets, supply chain disruptions, and unemployment.
- Potential for civil unrest and community fragmentation.

Pro Tip: Stay informed through reputable news sources, scientific reports, and local data to track emerging trends and risks.

Step 2: Innovate for Sustainability

Incorporating cutting-edge technologies and practices can enhance your ability to adapt and thrive.

1. Embrace Renewable Technologies:

- Upgrade to advanced solar panels or wind turbines for greater efficiency.
- Explore emerging energy sources, such as hydrogen fuel cells or geothermal systems.

2. Experiment with Advanced Agriculture:

- Use vertical farming or aquaponics to grow food in limited spaces.
- Incorporate drought-resistant crops and soil regeneration techniques.

3. Invest in Water Recycling Systems:

- Install greywater recycling systems to reuse household water for irrigation.
- Harvest and purify rainwater for potable and non-potable uses.

Innovation	Benefit	Cost Range
Advanced Solar Panels	Higher energy output	$200–$400 per panel
Vertical Farming Units	Space-efficient food production	$1,000–$5,000
Greywater Recycling	Reduces water waste	$500–$2,000

Real-Life Example: A suburban home in California integrated vertical farming and greywater recycling, reducing their water consumption by 40% and producing fresh greens year-round.

Step 3: Build Collaborative Networks

Strengthening ties with neighbors and like-minded individuals amplifies your efforts and ensures collective resilience.

1. Form Cooperative Groups:

- Establish resource-sharing networks for tools, seeds, and equipment.
- Create community gardens to increase local food security.

2. Participate in Knowledge Exchange:

- Host skill-sharing workshops on topics like permaculture or renewable energy.
- Collaborate on research projects to test and refine sustainable practices.

3. Advocate for Local Policy Change:

- Support initiatives that promote renewable energy, urban farming, and water conservation.
- Engage with local government to secure funding or incentives for sustainable projects.

Collaboration Method	Outcome	Example Initiative
Resource Sharing	Reduced costs, increased access	Tool libraries
Community Gardens	Improved food security	Vacant lot transformation
Policy Advocacy	Long-term systemic change	Renewable energy subsidies

Pro Tip: Use social media platforms or apps like Nextdoor to organize and mobilize your community.

Step 4: Prioritize Environmental Stewardship

Protecting natural resources ensures a sustainable future for both your household and the planet.

1. Minimize Waste:

- Compost food scraps and yard waste to create nutrient-rich soil.
- Reduce single-use plastics by switching to reusable alternatives.

2. Restore Local Ecosystems:

- Plant native species to support biodiversity and reduce water usage.
- Remove invasive plants and promote pollinator-friendly habitats.

3. Monitor Your Carbon Footprint:

- Transition to electric vehicles or carpooling to reduce emissions.
- Use energy-efficient appliances and insulate your home to lower heating and cooling demands.

Stewardship Action	Impact	Implementation
Composting	Reduces landfill waste	Home compost bins
Native Planting	Supports biodiversity	Local plant nurseries
Insulation Upgrades	Cuts energy consumption	Professional installation

Real-Life Example: A family in Oregon restored a portion of their property to native prairie, attracting pollinators and reducing irrigation needs by 30%.

Step 5: Plan for Future Generations

Sustainability is a legacy that benefits those who come after you.

1. Document Your Systems:

- Create detailed guides and diagrams for maintaining and replicating your self-sufficient systems.
- Store this information digitally and in physical formats to ensure accessibility.

2. Involve Younger Generations:

- Teach children and teens the principles of sustainability through hands-on activities.
- Encourage innovative thinking and problem-solving to adapt systems to future challenges.

3. Support Educational Programs:

- Partner with schools or local organizations to promote sustainability education.
- Donate resources or volunteer to mentor young learners.

Legacy Action	Benefit	Example Activity
System Documentation	Ensures continuity	Manuals, videos
Youth Engagement	Fosters next-gen leaders	Workshops, mentorship
Education Support	Expands community knowledge	School partnerships

Pro Tip: Establish a family or community fund dedicated to sustainability projects, ensuring resources for future initiatives.

Preparing for a sustainable future is an ongoing journey that combines innovation, collaboration, and stewardship. By anticipating challenges, embracing new technologies, and fostering a culture of resilience, you create a legacy of sustainability that endures through generations. As you continue to refine and expand your efforts, remember that every action you take contributes to a brighter, more sustainable tomorrow.

Rebuilding for a Resilient Future

While initial recovery efforts focus on stabilizing and meeting immediate needs, true resilience is built in the aftermath. The next step is about transforming your recovery into an opportunity for long-term improvement. By systematically rebuilding and incorporating lessons learned, you ensure your household and community are better prepared for future challenges. This guide provides actionable steps to upgrade systems, strengthen emotional and social networks, and build a robust foundation for enduring resilience.

Step 1: Assess the Damage

A thorough assessment helps prioritize recovery efforts and allocate resources effectively.

1. Inspect Your Property:

- Check for structural damage to your home, including roofs, walls, and foundations.
- Evaluate your water, energy, and food systems for functionality.

2. Inventory Losses:

- Document damaged or lost items with photos and detailed descriptions.
- Categorize losses into immediate needs (e.g., clean water) and long-term replacements (e.g., solar panels).

3. Consult Professionals:

- Hire experts to inspect critical systems, such as electrical wiring or plumbing, to ensure safety.
- Seek advice on rebuilding efficiently and sustainably.

Area	Inspection Focus	Action Needed
Structural Integrity	Roofs, walls, foundation	Repair or reinforce
Energy Systems	Solar panels, generators	Test, repair, or replace
Water Systems	Storage tanks, filters	Clean, repair, or upgrade

Pro Tip: Create a prioritized checklist to tackle immediate hazards before addressing cosmetic or non-essential repairs.

Step 2: Secure Essential Needs

Meeting basic needs ensures stability during the recovery period.

1. Water and Food Supply:

- Use stored water or purify available sources until your primary system is operational.
- Rely on preserved foods and quickly reestablish your garden or livestock systems.

2. Temporary Shelter:

- Set up tents, tarps, or designated safe rooms if your home is uninhabitable.
- Use portable heating or cooling devices to maintain comfort.

3. Communication and Power:

- Deploy portable power stations, battery backups, or generators for essential devices.
- Use two-way radios or satellite phones to stay connected if traditional networks are down.

Essential Need	Solution	Implementation
Drinking Water	Portable filters, purification	Lifestraw, chlorine tablets
Food	Preserved stockpile	Rotate canned or dried goods
Shelter	Temporary structures	Tents, tarps

Real-Life Example: A family in Texas used their emergency water storage and a portable generator to maintain basic functions during a prolonged power outage, avoiding the need to relocate.

Step 3: Develop a Recovery Plan

A clear plan ensures efficient resource use and reduces stress during rebuilding.

1. Set Short- and Long-Term Goals:

- **Short-Term:** Restore safety, secure essentials, and stabilize systems.
- **Long-Term:** Rebuild stronger systems, replenish supplies, and enhance resilience.

2. Allocate Resources Wisely:

- Focus funds and efforts on critical repairs and upgrades.
- Use community resources or government assistance programs to offset costs.

3. Monitor Progress:

- Schedule regular check-ins to evaluate milestones and adjust plans as needed.
- Keep detailed records of repairs, expenses, and system upgrades.

Goal Type	Example Action	Timeline
Short-Term	Repair roof, clean water system	Within 1–2 weeks
Long-Term	Install advanced solar panels	1–3 months
Continuous Improvement	Conduct regular system tests	Ongoing

Pro Tip: Break large tasks into smaller, actionable steps to avoid feeling overwhelmed.

Step 4: Foster Emotional and Mental Recovery

Recovering from a crisis is not just about physical rebuilding; mental well-being is equally important.

1. Provide Emotional Support:

- Encourage open communication within your family to share fears, frustrations, and ideas.
- Seek professional counseling if stress or trauma persists.

2. Reestablish Routines:

- Resume daily schedules, such as meal times and chores, to create a sense of normalcy.
- Incorporate recreational activities to boost morale and reduce tension.

3. Connect with Others:

- Join local support groups or online forums to share experiences and gain advice.
- Volunteer in community recovery efforts to foster a sense of purpose and connection.

Real-Life Example: After a wildfire, a community in California organized weekly potlucks to share resources and support one another, accelerating both physical and emotional recovery.

Step 5: Build Back Better

Use the recovery period as an opportunity to improve your systems and increase resilience.

1. Upgrade Systems:

- Replace damaged components with more durable, efficient alternatives.
- Consider redundancies for critical resources, such as dual water filtration systems or backup generators.

2. Incorporate Lessons Learned:

- Document what worked well and what didn't during the crisis.
- Adjust preparedness plans to address identified weaknesses.

3. Strengthen Community Bonds:

- Collaborate with neighbors to create shared resources, such as emergency supply depots.
- Develop a neighborhood recovery plan for future crises.

System Improvement	Benefit	Example Upgrade
Energy Resilience	Reliable power during outages	Add battery storage
Water Security	Extended access to clean water	Install larger storage tanks
Structural Integrity	Minimized future damage	Reinforce roofing materials

Pro Tip: Take advantage of recovery grants or insurance payouts to invest in long-lasting upgrades.

Crisis recovery is an opportunity to rebuild with greater strength and foresight. By assessing damage, securing essentials, fostering emotional resilience, and incorporating lessons learned, you can turn adversity into an opportunity for growth. Remember, recovery is a journey—approach it with patience, adaptability, and a commitment to continuous improvement.

Chapter 23: Cybersecurity for Home Defense

Protecting Your Digital Fortress

In today's interconnected world, your home's defense is not complete without securing its digital counterpart. Smart technologies, from internet-connected cameras to automated locks, bring convenience but also expose vulnerabilities that cybercriminals can exploit. Much like reinforcing a physical door or window, fortifying your home's digital infrastructure is essential for safeguarding your family and personal data. Think of cybersecurity as your virtual perimeter defense, ensuring that every connected device remains secure from outside threats.

Common Cybersecurity Threats

Phishing Attacks, Malware, and Ransomware

- **Phishing Attacks:** Cybercriminals use deceptive emails or messages to trick you into providing sensitive information like passwords or credit card details. These often appear to come from trusted sources.
- **Malware and Ransomware:** Malware infiltrates devices through downloads or malicious websites, while ransomware locks your files until a payment is made, often demanding cryptocurrency.

Risks from Unsecured Smart Devices

- **Cameras and Locks:** Hackers can gain access to live feeds or override locks if devices are not properly secured.
- **Thermostats and Other IoT Devices:** Compromised devices can be used as entry points to your network or for launching larger cyberattacks.

Data Theft and Financial Fraud

- **Identity Theft:** Cybercriminals can steal personal information to impersonate you, drain accounts, or open fraudulent lines of credit.
- **Financial Fraud:** Breached accounts can lead to unauthorized transactions, impacting financial stability and trust.

Building Digital Defenses

Creating Strong Passwords and Using Password Managers

- **Strong Passwords:** Use a mix of uppercase, lowercase, numbers, and symbols. Avoid easily guessed words like names or birthdates.
    - Example: Replace "Password123" with something like "P@55w0rd!897."
- **Password Managers:** Tools like LastPass or Dashlane can securely store and autofill unique passwords for every account, reducing reliance on memory.

Setting Up a VPN

- **Virtual Private Network (VPN):** A VPN encrypts your internet connection, making it difficult for hackers to intercept data. It also masks your IP address, adding another layer of privacy.
    - Use reputable services like NordVPN or ExpressVPN for maximum protection.

Installing and Updating Firewalls and Antivirus Software

- **Firewalls:** Act as a barrier between your devices and potential threats, blocking unauthorized access.
    - Many routers come with built-in firewalls; ensure they are enabled.
- **Antivirus Software:** Regularly update antivirus programs to protect against new threats. Look for trusted brands like Norton, McAfee, or Bitdefender.

Securing IoT Devices

- **Change Default Settings:** Update factory-set passwords on all devices.
- **Update Firmware:** Regularly check for and apply updates to keep devices secure against newly discovered vulnerabilities.
- **Network Segmentation:** Create a separate Wi-Fi network for smart devices to isolate them from computers or phones with sensitive data.

Recognizing and Responding to Threats

How to Identify Phishing Attempts and Suspicious Activities

- **Signs of Phishing:**
    - Messages urging immediate action, such as "Your account will be locked in 24 hours."
    - Poor grammar or formatting in emails claiming to be from reputable companies.
    - Links that redirect to unfamiliar websites.
- **Suspicious Activities:**
    - Unusual account activity notifications from banks or email providers.
    - Devices operating slower than normal or displaying unexpected pop-ups.

Steps to Take During a Cybersecurity Breach

1. **Isolate Compromised Devices:**
   - Disconnect the device from Wi-Fi or turn off its internet connection to prevent further infiltration.
2. **Change Passwords:**
   - Use a secure, uncompromised device to change passwords for affected accounts.
3. **Scan for Malware:**
   - Use antivirus software to identify and remove malicious files or programs.
4. **Inform Relevant Parties:**
   - Notify your bank or credit card provider if financial information is at risk.
   - Report breaches to the device manufacturer if an IoT system is compromised.

Resources for Monitoring and Reporting Threats

- **Monitoring:**
  - Services like Have I Been Pwned help you check if your accounts have been part of data breaches.
  - Use network monitoring tools like Fing to detect unauthorized devices on your home network.
- **Reporting:**
  - Report cybercrime to local authorities or dedicated agencies such as the FBI's Internet Crime Complaint Center (IC3) in the U.S.
  - Contact your Internet Service Provider (ISP) for support in addressing network-level attacks.

Pro Tip: Schedule monthly cybersecurity checkups to review settings, update devices, and ensure all systems are operating with the latest security protocols. These small, consistent actions can significantly reduce vulnerabilities and keep your digital fortress secure.

Chapter 24: Fitness and Training for Preparedness

Introduction: Strength and Resilience for Survival

Physical fitness is often overlooked in preparedness planning but remains one of the most critical factors in survival. Strength, endurance, and agility enable you to react effectively in emergencies, whether escaping danger, carrying supplies, or defending your home. This chapter explores tailored fitness routines and training strategies to enhance your preparedness, focusing on functional strength and tactical readiness.

The Role of Fitness in Preparedness
Why Physical Fitness Matters

- **Mobility:** Navigate obstacles, climb, or run when necessary.
- **Strength:** Lift heavy items like emergency kits, furniture for barricades, or injured individuals.
- **Endurance:** Sustain prolonged physical activity during evacuations or long-term tasks.
- **Stress Management:** Exercise reduces anxiety and sharpens decision-making during high-stress scenarios.

Designing a Preparedness Fitness Plan
Key Components of a Balanced Routine

1. **Strength Training:**
    - Focus on compound movements like squats, deadlifts, and push-ups to build core strength.
    - Incorporate weighted carries, such as farmer's walks, to mimic real-world tasks.
2. **Cardiovascular Endurance:**
    - Train with running, cycling, or swimming to improve stamina.
    - Practice interval training to develop the ability to switch between intense bursts and recovery periods.
3. **Flexibility and Mobility:**
    - Perform dynamic stretches and yoga to maintain joint health and prevent injuries.
    - Include exercises like hip openers and shoulder stretches for better range of motion.
4. **Tactical Skills:**
    - Simulate emergency scenarios like carrying a loaded backpack or climbing over obstacles.
    - Practice self-defense drills to build confidence and reaction time.

Preparedness-Specific Workouts
Functional Training Routine

Frequency: 3–4 times per week

Warm-Up:

- Jumping jacks – 3 minutes
- Dynamic stretches (arm circles, lunges) – 5 minutes

Workout:

- Farmer's Carry: Walk 50 meters with heavy weights in both hands (3 sets).
- Push-Ups: 15–20 reps (3 sets).
- Box Jumps or Step-Ups: 10–15 reps (3 sets).
- Plank: Hold for 1 minute (3 sets).
- Sprints: 30-second sprint, 90-second rest (5 rounds).

Cool-Down:

- Static stretches focusing on hamstrings, shoulders, and back – 5–10 minutes.

Real-Life Training Scenarios
Scenario 1: Bug-Out Practice

- **Task:** Simulate a rapid evacuation with a loaded backpack weighing 20–40 pounds.
- **Objective:** Cover 1–3 miles within a specific time frame, including obstacles like stairs or uneven terrain.

Scenario 2: Defensive Position Drills

- **Task:** Practice moving between cover points with speed and agility.
- **Objective:** Build muscle memory for quick reaction and efficient use of space in emergencies.

Scenario 3: Lifting and Carrying

- **Task:** Practice lifting and carrying heavy objects such as sandbags or water containers.
- **Objective:** Develop the strength to handle physically demanding tasks during disasters.

Monitoring Progress and Staying Motivated
Tracking Fitness Improvements

- **Strength Gains:** Track weights lifted and reps completed.
- **Endurance Milestones:** Measure running or walking distances over time.
- **Skill Development:** Evaluate performance in simulated emergency drills.

Staying Committed

- **Set Goals:** Define specific objectives, like completing a 5K run or lifting a certain weight.
- **Mix It Up:** Rotate workouts to prevent boredom and target different muscle groups.
- **Involve Others:** Train with family or friends to build camaraderie and accountability.

Pro Tip: Every small improvement in fitness can significantly enhance your survival odds in a crisis. Regularly update your fitness plan to align with your evolving preparedness needs.

4-Week Preparedness Fitness Plan

Overview:
This plan is designed to build strength, endurance, flexibility, and tactical skills relevant to emergency preparedness. Workouts are scalable based on fitness level, with options to increase intensity or modify exercises as needed.

Week 1: Foundation Building

Focus: Establishing baseline strength, endurance, and mobility.

Day 1: Strength Training

- Warm-Up:
    - Jumping jacks – 2 minutes
    - Arm and leg swings – 10 reps per side
- Main Workout:
    - Bodyweight Squats – 3 sets of 12–15 reps
    - Push-Ups – 3 sets of 10–15 reps
    - Plank – 3 rounds of 30 seconds hold
    - Farmer's Carry – 50 meters with light weights (e.g., water jugs), 3 sets
- Cool-Down:
    - Hamstring stretch – 30 seconds per side
    - Child's pose – 1 minute

Day 2: Cardio and Agility

- Warm-Up:
    - High knees – 2 minutes
    - Dynamic lunges – 10 reps per leg
- Main Workout:
    - Interval Training:
        - Sprint for 30 seconds, walk for 90 seconds (repeat 6 rounds)
    - Side Shuffles – 10 meters each side, 3 rounds
    - Step-Ups on a sturdy surface – 3 sets of 10 reps per leg
- Cool-Down:
    - Quad stretch – 30 seconds per side

- Forward fold – 1 minute

Day 3: Rest or Light Activity

- Activities: Gentle yoga, walking, or stretching.

Day 4: Tactical Strength and Drills

- Warm-Up:
  - Arm circles and hip rotations – 2 minutes
  - Light jogging – 3 minutes
- Main Workout:
  - Sandbag Lifting: Lift and carry a sandbag (20–40 lbs) for 20 meters, 3 rounds
  - Push-Ups – 3 sets of 12–15 reps
  - Defensive Movement Drill: Move between two cover points (e.g., behind furniture) at speed, 5 rounds
  - Plank with Shoulder Taps – 3 sets of 15 taps per side
- Cool-Down:
  - Cat-cow stretches – 1 minute
  - Hamstring stretch – 30 seconds per leg

Day 5: Endurance Challenge

- Activity: Walk or hike 2–3 miles with a backpack (15–20 lbs).
- Cool-Down: Stretch major muscle groups after completion.

Day 6: Functional Mobility and Recovery

- Activities: Yoga session focusing on hip openers, hamstring stretches, and spinal mobility.

Day 7: Rest or Light Activity

- Options: Leisure walk, light stretching.

Week 2: Progression

Adjustments: Increase intensity by adding weight or reps to strength exercises and reducing rest periods during cardio intervals.

- Add 5 lbs to weighted carries or sandbags.
- Sprint for 45 seconds instead of 30 seconds.

Week 3: Tactical Training

Focus: Simulate emergency scenarios.

Day 1:

- Bug-Out Simulation: Walk 3 miles with a backpack weighing 20–30 lbs.
- Defensive Drill: Move between cover points, adding 10 push-ups at each point (5 rounds).

Day 2:

- Strength Circuit:
    - Deadlifts (using a sandbag or weights) – 3 sets of 10 reps
    - Pull-Ups (or assisted pull-ups) – 3 sets of 5–8 reps
    - Plank to Push-Up – 3 sets of 10 reps

Day 3: Rest or Light Activity

Day 4:

- Agility and Reaction:
    - Shuttle Runs: Sprint 10 meters, touch the ground, and return, 5 rounds
    - Reaction Drill: Partner calls out movements (e.g., "duck," "run," "cover"), responding immediately (10 minutes).

Week 4: Peak Challenge

Goal: Test endurance and strength with combined drills.

Day 1:

- Circuit Challenge:
    - Farmer's Carry: 100 meters with 30–40 lbs
    - Push-Ups – 20 reps
    - Sprint – 50 meters
    - Repeat circuit 5 times

Day 3:

- Tactical Movement:
    - Move through simulated obstacles (e.g., climb over low walls, crawl under tables).

Day 5:

- Bug-Out Challenge:
    - Walk or hike 5 miles with a fully loaded backpack (20–40 lbs).

Notes on Progress:

- **Track Improvements:** Record weights, times, and distances weekly.
- **Modify for Safety:** Adjust intensity based on fitness level or physical limitations.
- **Hydration and Nutrition:** Stay hydrated and eat balanced meals to support recovery.

Chapter 25: Expanding Defense to Vehicles

Mobile Security as a Strategic Asset

Your vehicle is more than just a means of transportation—it's an essential part of your home defense strategy. From securing it against theft to utilizing it for evacuation or temporary shelter, ensuring your vehicle is ready for any emergency can provide mobility, safety, and self-reliance. This chapter explores strategies for vehicle security, preparation, and effective use in crisis situations.

Securing Your Vehicle

Vehicles are a common target for theft and can also be vulnerable during emergencies. Protecting them is essential for mobility and safety.

1. Physical Security Measures:

- **Steering Wheel Locks:** Deter theft by immobilizing the steering wheel.
- **GPS Tracking Systems:** Install trackers to locate your vehicle if stolen.
- **Car Alarms:** Ensure alarms are functional and include shock sensors for added protection.

2. Parking and Storage Tips:

- **At Home:** Park in a well-lit, secure location, preferably inside a garage.
- **In Public:** Choose spots near security cameras or high-traffic areas to reduce theft risk.

3. Emergency Lockdown Features:

- Use window tints or covers to obscure valuables.
- Install a kill switch to prevent unauthorized starting.

Preparing Your Vehicle for Emergencies

A prepared vehicle ensures you're ready to act during crises, from natural disasters to prolonged power outages.

1. Emergency Vehicle Kit:

Keep a fully stocked kit tailored to your location and potential emergencies.

- **Essentials:**
    - First aid supplies
    - Non-perishable snacks and water
    - Flashlight and extra batteries
- **Tools and Equipment:**
    - Jumper cables
    - Tire repair kit and portable air compressor
    - Multitool or basic tool kit

2. Fuel and Energy Management:

- Maintain at least half a tank of fuel at all times.
- Store additional fuel safely in approved containers.
- For electric vehicles, keep them charged to at least 80% whenever possible.

3. Navigation and Communication Tools:

- Equip vehicles with physical maps in case GPS services fail.
- Include a CB radio or portable two-way radios for off-grid communication.

Using Vehicles as Part of Your Defense Strategy

In emergencies, your vehicle can be an invaluable asset for evacuation or as a temporary base of operations.

1. Evacuation Readiness:

- **Pre-Route Planning:** Map out multiple evacuation routes and identify key resources along the way (e.g., gas stations, rest areas).
- **Load-Out Efficiency:** Keep your vehicle organized for quick loading of essential supplies.

2. Vehicles as Temporary Shelters:

- Use car seats and insulation materials to create a comfortable sleeping area.
- Consider solar window shades or portable fans for temperature regulation.

3. Defensive Mobility:

- In civil unrest or dangerous scenarios, maintain mobility to avoid becoming trapped.
- Use your vehicle to create barriers or block access points as needed.

Maintenance and Long-Term Preparation

Regular upkeep ensures your vehicle remains reliable during emergencies.

1. Regular Maintenance Checks:

- Inspect tires, brakes, and fluid levels monthly.
- Keep spare parts such as fuses, hoses, and belts on hand.

2. Seasonal Preparations:

- In winter, carry chains, ice scrapers, and blankets.
- In summer, pack extra water, coolant, and sun protection materials.

3. Long-Term Storage Tips:

- Use fuel stabilizers to prevent gasoline from degrading.
- Disconnect the battery if the vehicle will sit idle for extended periods.

Real-Life Example

During a wildfire evacuation, a family in California relied on their vehicle as both transport and shelter. Their pre-packed emergency kit, full gas tank, and detailed route plan allowed them to evacuate quickly and find safety. They used their vehicle's power to charge communication devices and its interior as a safe resting place during extended roadblocks.

Incorporating vehicles into your defense strategy enhances your flexibility and ability to respond to crises. By securing your car, equipping it with essential supplies, and planning for contingencies, you ensure that your vehicle remains a reliable tool for safety and survival.

Conclusion: A Legacy of Resilience and Preparedness

The journey to building a secure, self-sufficient, and resilient lifestyle is not a destination but a lifelong commitment. This book has provided you with the tools, strategies, and insights needed to protect your home, family, and community in the face of uncertainty. From fortifying your property and mastering cybersecurity to fostering physical preparedness and creating sustainable systems, you now have a comprehensive framework to handle a wide range of challenges.

Preparedness Is Empowerment

Preparedness is about more than just surviving crises—it's about thriving despite them. It's the confidence that comes from knowing you've planned for the unexpected, the peace of mind that comes with protecting your loved ones, and the satisfaction of living in harmony with the resources around you. This mindset empowers you to approach the future with optimism, adaptability, and strength.

Beyond the Individual: Building a Culture of Resilience

True preparedness goes beyond individual households. It's about inspiring and empowering others to take action, strengthening communities, and creating a culture of resilience. By sharing your knowledge, collaborating with neighbors, and advocating for sustainable practices, you contribute to a world where more people are equipped to face challenges together.

A Future Ready for Anything

The world is constantly changing, and new threats will emerge alongside new opportunities. Stay curious, stay informed, and continue to adapt your strategies as technology evolves and global circumstances shift. Your ability to anticipate and respond to challenges will ensure that your efforts not only protect your household but also leave a lasting legacy for future generations.

Unlock Exclusive Bonuses!

By scanning this QR code, you'll gain access to an array of invaluable resources specifically designed to <u>complement the strategies and insights from this book.</u>

What's inside?

- **The Ultimate Bug Out Bag Checklist** – Ensure you're fully prepared for any scenario.
- **50 PDF Guides on Alternate Energy** – Discover innovative ways to stay powered up during emergencies.
- **365 Essential Survival Skills** – Acquire vital knowledge that can truly keep you alive when it matters most.

These resources will help you elevate your preparedness and *take your home defense plan to the next level.*

Don't miss this opportunity—scan the QR code now and start exploring your bonus content!

A Personal Note of Thanks

Thank you for choosing to read *The Navy SEAL Ultimate Home Defense Playbook*. Your time, commitment, and dedication to securing your home and preparing for any scenario mean the world to me. I hope this guide has provided you with the tools, strategies, and confidence to protect what matters most.

If you found value in this book, I would greatly appreciate it if you could **leave a review on Amazon.**

Your feedback not only helps me improve future editions but also *assists others in discovering this guide and taking steps toward their own preparedness.*

Sharing your thoughts about what resonated with you—or how this book has made a difference in your approach to home defense—would be immensely helpful.

Together, we can **create a community of empowered and resilient individuals.**

Thank you for being a part of this mission.

Stay safe and prepared,

Jake

Made in the USA
Columbia, SC
20 April 2025